How to Eat like a Vegetarian
Even If You Never Want to Be One

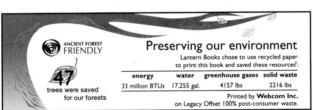

ANCIENT FOREST
FRIENDLY

47

trees were saved
for our forests

Preserving our environment

Lantern Books chose to use recycled paper
to print this book and saved these resources[1]:

energy	water	greenhouse gases	solid waste
33 million BTUs	17,255 gal.	4157 lbs	2216 lbs

Printed by **Webcom Inc.**
on Legacy Offset 100% post-consumer waste.

FSC

Recycled
Supporting responsible
use of forest resources

Cert no. SW-COC-002358
www.fsc.org
© 1996 Forest Stewardship Council

[1]Estimates were made using the Environmental Defense Paper Calculator.

As part of Lantern Books' commitment to the environment we have joined the Green Press Initiative, a nonprofit organization supporting publishers in using fiber that is not sourced from ancient or endangered forests.

For more information, visit www.greenpressinitiative.org

How to Eat like a Vegetarian Even If You Never Want to Be One

More than 250 Shortcuts, Strategies, and Simple Solutions

Carol J. Adams and Patti Breitman

Lantern Books ɔ New York
A Division of Booklight Inc.

2008
Lantern Books
A Division of Booklight Inc.
128 Second Place
Brooklyn, NY 11231

Printed in Canada

Library of Congress Cataloging-in-Publication Data

Adams, Carol J.
 How to eat like a vegetarian even if you never want to be one : more than 250 shortcuts, strategies, and simple solutions / Carol J. Adams and Patti Breitman.
     p. cm.
 Includes index.
 ISBN-13: 978-1-59056-137-9 (alk. paper)
 ISBN-10: 1-59056-137-6 (alk. paper)
  1. Vegetarianism. 2. Vegetarian cookery. I. Breitman, Patti, 1954– II. Title.
 TX392.A4135 2008
 641.5'636—dc22

                                  2008007395

Notes regarding permission to reprint recipes are found on page 206.

For all the writers and cooks
who help Patti and Carol eat like vegetarians,
and for our readers,
who are willing to test new ideas,
taste new tastes, and explore new options.
This book is for you, especially if you have ever told us:
"I would eat this way more often, if only. . . ."

Contents

❧

Expanded Table of Contents

◑

Introduction

Thanks for picking up this book! Whatever your reason for wanting to eat like a vegetarian, the fact that you are interested at all shows that you are open minded and caring. Maybe you want to cook for a vegetarian in your life. Maybe you want to cut down on the saturated fat, cholesterol, or calories in your diet. Maybe you want to eat more vegetables and just need some new ideas. Maybe you have thought that vegetarianism just takes too much time, but want to give it one more chance. No matter what attracted you, we are delighted to welcome you!

Based on our combined fifty-plus years as vegetarians, we know that anything new can seem intimidating. We know you are busy, and we don't intend to add hours of chopping and cooking to your busy lives. But we do intend to show you how to incorporate healthy, tasty vegetarian foods into your already full schedules. That is why the book starts with tips on food and cooking. Right off we want you to know this book speaks to you in your busy lives. We offer quick tips, easy meals, useful lists, and information, and we try to be brief because we know you do not have time to spare. We want to provide you with what you have been looking for—simple recipes, helpful ideas, and advice born of experience that can transform the way you eat. Before you know it, maybe even tonight, you will feel ready to enjoy delicious, easy-to-prepare foods from the plant kingdom.

After all the tips, hints, and recipes we will share what motivates us and what we hope will encourage and motivate you to put our strategies into action.

But we don't want to keep you from the easy steps to achieving this. Here's our first tip: try just one thing. It's your choice—examine the tips and think about what has concerned you: That you can't cook vegetarian because it means too much shopping and chopping? (Take a look at Ten Time-Saving Tips). Have you been postponing learning about kale or chard? (Take a look at Ten Ways to Eat More Dark, Leafy Greens.)

For years, our friends have told us, "We could be vegetarians if you prepared our meals for us." Now we are sharing our secrets—it doesn't take much cooking. It's simple, fast, and anyone can do it.

You don't have to become a vegetarian to include more health-promoting, plant-based foods in your diet. All you have to do is try one thing; simply start there. We hope this book will provide you with confidence and the tools to do just that.

Part One

Two Hundred (and More!) Ways to Eat like A Vegetarian

People who have been eating well as vegetarians don't spend a lot of time worrying about what they are going to eat, so if you are going to eat like them, that's the first thing—stop worrying. Wc have summarized what we have learned from our decades of vegetarianism, and made the following lists to help you discover the ease of eating like a vegetarian.

Ten Time-Saving Tips

1. Always have a fruit bowl in the kitchen so you can eat an apple, apricot, plum, pear, banana, or other fruit as you decide what to prepare.
2. If you don't have time to make a salad, don't make a salad. Serve raw vegetables (baby carrots, jicama, celery, red cabbage leaves) with salsa, guacamole, hummus, or another dip.
3. Prepare vegetables when you unpack your groceries rather than when you need them. Store washed veggies in a plastic or cloth bag (not sealed) or plastic or glass bin along with a paper or cloth napkin. Or buy vegetables pre-cut and ready to eat.
4. Always cook more grains than you think you need.
5. Buy canned beans and an electric can opener. Rinse beans in their own cans. Using the lid to hold the beans in, dump the water, then holding the lid on the whole time, refill with water, swish it around, dump that water. After a couple of times, you have rinsed your beans without a colander.
6. Prepare HUGE HUGE HUGE salads (include beans and lots of crunchy fresh veggies). Use pre-washed salad mix as a base. Add vegetables and/or fruit. Try any of these in any combination: red cabbage; red onions; dark, leafy greens; carrots; tomatoes; cucumbers; artichoke hearts (water packed); celery; yellow squash; zucchini; pears; orange slices; apples; corn; peas; snow peas; cauliflower; broccoli. Optional: Add nuts or avocado just before serving.
7. Make a huge pot of soup and add to it every day. Add a new veg-

etable to each portion every time you reheat it. Or create different soups with each reheating. Make a broth for one night. The second night, add potatoes and purée it and you have a creamy soup. The third night throw in lots of corn and broccoli and you have a chowder-like soup.

8. Use soup as a topping. Green or red gazpacho (see pages 58 and 60) can be a salad dressing and Jennifer's Lentil Barley Soup (see page 122) is a wonderful topping for baked potatoes or yams.

9. Learn how to make polenta. It is one of the fastest and most satisfying foods. It makes a beautiful presentation; it lasts well; it makes a great sandwich or main dish; and you can top it with pesto or sun-dried tomato paste from a jar or made from scratch (see pages 78 and 80).

10. Discover how easy it is to make hummus. It is one of the most versatile foods around. Use it as a dip, water it down with more lemon juice, lime juice or water, and it's a salad dressing. It's a terrific sandwich spread and a marvelously versatile stuffing for raw vegetables (see page 76).

Ten Ways to Eat More Vegetables

1. Don't wait until you're hungry to fix your vegetables. Create your own salad bar in the fridge, so you can quickly mix and match veggies for a snack or salad.

2. Grate zucchini or carrots into "angel hair pasta." A spiraling gadget or food processor does this easily.

3. Use collard greens, bok choy, or kale instead of lettuce on sandwiches.

4. Serve veggie chips (slices of carrot, jicama, green or red peppers, radishes, or celery) with all sandwiches and soups.

5. Include a salad with every lunch and dinner. Challenge yourself to make it as colorful as possible.

6. Discover some delicious dips and use florets of broccoli and cauliflower instead of greasy chips (see recipes on pages 76–80).

7. When eating out, ask what vegetables the chef can prepare without butter. Try new ethnic restaurants where vegetable-based dishes can take center stage (Thai, Chinese, Japanese, Indian, Italian, Mexican).

8. Become an expert on dark leafy greens: impress your family and friends with new recipes and new facts (see pages 8, 97, and 175).

9. Munch on red, yellow, or green peppers as you would an apple; munch on celery, jicama, and carrot sticks as you would a pretzel.

10. Use steamed and mashed broccoli and/or cauliflower instead of canned tuna fish for a tasty sandwich filler. Optional: add mustard or egg free mayo, pickle relish, and chopped celery.

Ten Ways to Eat More Legumes

1. Start with legumes like lentils, split peas, and chickpeas, which seem to be well-tolerated by most people.
2. Start eating a very little bit every day . . . toss them into a salad, or a soup. Try starting with small portions. Give your stomach time to acclimate. What passes as a normal portion in the United States is way too much for someone whose stomach is not used to eating beans. If you never eat beans your intestines are not yet comfortable digesting the protein and starch that come in one package in beans. And though they are good for you, some people don't tolerate them well at first. Start with only one or two tablespoons of cooked beans, give your stomach time to adapt, and your body will tell you when you can tolerate more of them.
3. After a week of split peas or lentils, start with larger beans, but very few.
4. Try canned beans. They save time and have the same nutrients as soaked and cooked dried beans. Rinse them well to remove excess salt.
5. Have a bean burrito.
6. Discover hummus. It's a versatile staple in many vegetarians' diets.
7. Use peanut butter instead of butter. Peanuts are not really nuts, but legumes.
8. Edamame are soybeans in their pods. Most Japanese restaurants

have them as appetizers. You can buy them frozen, in their pods or not. They are tasty!

9. Try pasta faggiole—a popular pasta-and-bean combination in many menus and Italian restaurants. Or try minestrone, often made with fava beans and many vegetables.

10. Learn to make a fast black bean dip. Add some salsa from a jar if you want it *picante*.

Ten Ways to Eat More Dark, Leafy Greens

1. Steam leafy greens. Add toasted sesame seeds that you toasted in a toaster oven. Season with a drop or two of seasoned rice vinegar or soy sauce.
2. Always add dark, leafy greens to salads. While an entire salad of raw kale or mustard greens might seem bitter, a few chopped leaves among the lettuce and other raw veggies are delicious.
3. Forget the lettuce on sandwiches and use leafy greens instead.
4. Add leafy greens to soups and stews in the last few minutes of cooking.
5. Make a dark, green soup by boiling an onion and two peeled diced potatoes until soft and then adding a bunch or two of collards and/or kale. Add a teaspoon each of marjoram and sage plus a dash of salt and pepper. When the greens are bright green (about 5 minutes in the broth), purée the whole mixture in small batches in the blender.
6. As you reheat leftover foods, consider adding a few leaves of kale, collards, or a few broccoli florets.
7. Use leafy greens as an edible doily when serving dips and vegetables.
8. Add raw or lightly steamed broccoli florets to pasta primavera, raw veggie platters, and salads.
9. Make a collard green–peanut butter roll: Wash a collard leaf and cut the stem out, resulting in two half leaves. Shake them or pat them dry, smear peanut butter on each one. Roll it up with peanut butter

on the inside. Cut into individual rolls like sushi or eat in whole as a roll up.

10. Discover arugula. It's a strongly flavored leafy green that adds bite to any salad or sandwich.

How to Fix Leafy Greens

Before eating or cooking kale or collard greens, you will want to first remove the bottom part of the woody stems. There are at least two ways to do this:

1. Use a sharp knife along each side of the stem or
2. Slide your hand up the stem, tearing the leafy part from the stem as you go. This works best if you start the "slide" by tearing a quarter inch of leaf on both sides of the stem first.

Steam leafy greens briefly over water. Sauté with chopped garlic in a tiny bit of olive oil or white wine or diluted apple juice.

Braise: Heat a heavy-duty saucepan over medium heat. Wash and chop leaves and add wet leaves to hot pot. They will first steam and then braise. You can add a little wine or mirin (Japanese sweet cooking wine) or balsamic vinegar or olive oil, but just a dash for flavor. Also you can add chopped garlic or toasted sesame seeds or garbanzo beans to taste. Stir once or twice while cooking, scraping the bottom of the pot. Cook 5 to 10 minutes.

Ten Ways to Adapt Your Favorite Recipes

◑

1. Instead of spaghetti and meat sauce:
   - spaghetti and marinara sauce
   - spaghetti with texturized vegetable protein (it's in the frozen department of grocery stores now, Morningside Farms Crumbles or Boca Burgers . . . add it to tomato sauce and warm).
2. Instead of a stir fry with meat, substitute tofu. A stir fry is still a stir fry.
3. Instead of a tuna salad sandwich:
   - Substitute tempeh, a fermented soybean product available in natural foods store. Steam it for twenty minutes, let it cool, and then use it instead of tuna and follow your recipe.
   - Steam cauliflower or broccoli for longer than you would usually steam them, until they are mushy, a good 10 to 15 minutes. Then mash them with a fork. Add chopped celery, a little bit of prepared mustard, chopped pickles, and eggless mayonnaise.
   - Use cooked or canned garbanzo beans; process them in a food processor and use them instead of tuna. Add chopped celery and dill (fresh or dried) and a little bit of prepared mustard, some capers, lemon juice.
4. Instead of a Reuben sandwich: Substitute tempeh or an avocado for the meat in a Reuben sandwich. (Steam tempeh for 20 minutes before using in a sandwich.)
5. Instead of Baked beans and "franks": Vegetarian baked beans and "not dogs." Use one can vegetarian baked beans, three vegan "hot

dogs," about 2 cups of sauerkraut and some prepared mustard. Heat the beans and "not dogs" in a pot. Add a tablespoon (or more to taste) of mustard. Serve over sauerkraut.

6. There are now commercial products that substitute for macaroni and cheese. Or check out Mac Daddy (see page 109).

7. Try tofu lasagna (see page 98).

8. Instead of scrambled eggs, try scrambled tofu. Buy firm tofu (not silken) and add to sautéed green onions, mushrooms, spinach, and any other vegetables. A pinch of turmeric will turn the tofu yellow (see page 47).

9. Many soups can become vegetarian simply by using vegetable stock instead of beef or chicken stock.

10. Instead of cereal with milk, try cereal with rice milk, soymilk, or nut milk.

Ten Ways to Add a New Food to Your Diet

1. Think of what you are doing not as leaving anything out of your diet but letting in new and valuable foods.

2. To try a new vegetable, either decide in advance which food you will try or go to the store and select a vegetable you have never used before.

3. Don't refrigerate it! Keeping it unrefrigerated will encourage you to use it soon after bringing it home, while you are motivated to experiment.

4. If you don't know how to cook it or whether you can eat it raw, search on that vegetable's name and "vegan" on Google, Dogpile, or any other Internet search engine.

5. Next time you are choosing a restaurant, try a vegetarian or ethnic place. See what you like among the abundant vegetarian choices.

6. Visit a library or bookstore and discover some new vegetarian cookbooks. Most now have an entire section devoted to vegetarian recipe books.

7. Have a potluck dinner at your house and ask your guests to bring a vegetarian dish and recipe.

8. Visit a farmer's market or talk to the produce manager at your grocery store. Ask for ideas on how to prepare a new vegetable.

9. Choose one new recipe each week that calls for a food you're not familiar with.

10. Make a familiar salad, but add one new ingredient.

Ten Tips for Making Fast Foods

1. Always have kale and cooked grains ready to heat up and eat.
2. Take tahini and yesterday's salad—blend them with water and/or lemon juice and serve over steamed vegetables.
3. Gussy up your leftovers. Whatever you had for dinner last night can become new for lunch today. Add some greens or sesame seeds. Or roll it up in a tortilla and top with salsa.
4. Buy flavored tofu to add to salads, or make your own: Marinate thin strips or small cubes of firm tofu in Bragg's Liquid Aminos or Low Sodium Soy Sauce with a little orange juice and grated ginger and crushed garlic. Then bake the tofu for 30 minutes on the tray of the toaster oven and add to salads or steamed vegetables.
5. Create a "deli" in your kitchen, so you can choose already prepared, health-promoting food. Prepare a few different salads (see pages 49–55) and have olives on hand.
6. A fruit plate is always a good lunch. Be sure to eat enough to sate your appetite. Adding a few sticks of celery or a few leaves of romaine lettuce will help fill you up.
7. Miso soup can be made in less than five minutes (see page 61).
8. A dressing can be as simple as Bragg's Liquid Aminos, or seasoned rice vinegar, each alone or in combination.
9. Top a baked potato with mashed avocado, or black beans out of a can, salsa out of a jar, or any leftover soup.
10. For an easy lunch, peel a garnet yam, cut it up, and steam it in a

steamer basket. After 10 minutes, add about six leaves of collard greens, chopped. When those are bright green (about two minutes more), transfer the yam/collard mix to a serving bowl, or roll up in a tortilla. Top it with garlic gomasio (a mix of salt, sesame seeds, and garlic).

Ten Fast Snacks or Easy Lunches

1. Tahini and celery.
2. Nut butter on a cracker or rice cakes.
3. Jam on whole wheat toast.
4. Spread mustard or vegan mayonnaise, nut butter, chutney, or hoisin sauce on a tortilla or chapatti. Top with any shredded or chopped veggies or mashed leftovers, and roll them up to be eaten by hand.
5. Spread instant beans on tortillas or chapattis and add any of the following: salsa, rice, sprouts, lettuce, dark greens, avocado, red or yellow or green peppers, shredded red cabbage.
6. Quick fruit smoothie: Toss a banana and any chopped fruit (except melon) in a blender with water or juice or soymilk.
7. Avocado sandwich with lettuce or kale, tomato and vegan mayo.
8. Leftover dinner! Leftovers are the fastest meal there is, so be sure to make more than you think you can eat for dinner.
9. Miso soup is fast, healthy, and versatile. Just pour boiling water over 1 to 2 teaspoons miso in a mug. You can add any chopped vegetable or small cubes of tofu if you want.
10. Instant mashed potatoes.

Ten Different Things You Can Do with Chickpeas

1. Make hummus (see page 76 for recipe).
2. Add more lemon juice or lime juice to hummus and turn it into a salad dressing.
3. Warm chickpeas in a toaster oven, sprinkle on some pepper, and snack on them instead of popcorn.
4. Add them to green salads.
5. Make "cheese" from them (see recipe page 72).
6. They are great in soups, especially Jennifer Raymond's cabbage and chickpea soup (see page 62).
7. Mash them. They add a nice texture to the many dishes, like casseroles.
8. Anytime you are making Indian food like red lentils, toss in garbanzo beans.
9. Use them as a garnish: place garbanzo beans around the edge of a dish to form an edible border.
10. Add them instead of—or in addition to—any of the beans in a three-bean salad.

Ten Top Vegetarian Convenience Foods

1. Instant hummus.
2. Canned beans.
3. Vegetable broth. (Canned or powder that you add to water; Patti likes Seitenbacher brand powder.)
4. Canned organic tomatoes: diced and whole, seasoned (Mexican and Italian), and stewed.
5. Instant mashed potatoes. Use them to thicken soups or bind a veggie burger.
6. Frozen vegetables.
7. Instant beans. Add water and you have refried beans or black beans.
8. Curry paste. Add to sautéed veggies and lentils and voila! instant curry.
9. Tomato sauce in jar.
10. Salad dressings.

Ten Uses for Your Favorite Salsa

1. As a dip, of course.
2. Instead of salad dressing on a salad.
3. Mix with silken tofu for a dip for veggies.
4. Mix with mashed avocado for a quick guacamole dip.
5. Use as a topping on beans.
6. Mix 3/4 cup salsa in a food processor with 1 can drained pinto beans, some fresh cilantro, a clove of garlic and some hot sauce, for a great dip.
7. Grill some veggies and top with salsa.
8. Add to instant refried beans or black beans and you have a dip.
9. Mix with vegan cream cheese and make a sandwich with it.
10. Use it as a topping with a wrap.

Ten Substitutes for Using an Egg in Baking

1. If it's just one egg being left out of a baked good, just leave it out. Add 2 tablespoons liquid.
2. Two tablespoons cornstarch added to the dry ingredients, and 2 tablespoons water to the wet ingredients.
3. One tablespoon Ener-G Egg Replacer (available at natural food stores) with two tablespoons water.
4. Two tablespoons arrowroot flour.
5. Two tablespoons potato starch.
6. One tablespoon flax seed and three tablespoons water. Blend flax seeds in blender, then add water. Blend for one to two minutes till mixture is thick and a little goo-ey.
7. One banana plus 1/2 teaspoon aluminum-free baking powder.
8. 1/4 cup silken, firm, or extra-firm tofu, puréed.
9. 1/4 cup applesauce plus 1/2 teaspoon aluminum-free baking powder.
10. Two tablespoons nut butter (peanut, almond, or tahini).

Ten Protein-Rich Vegetarian Foods

1. Veggie burgers.
2. Peanut butter.
3. Soymilk.
4. Beans.
5. Tofu.
6. Hummus.
7. Lentils.
8. Broccoli, cauliflower, bean sprouts.
9. Potatoes.
10. Veggie "meats".

Ten (Plus Five) Things to Keep in Your Pantry

⬤

1. The basics: onions, celery, and carrots.
2. A variety of vinegars (apple cider vinegar, balsamic vinegar, raspberry-flavored vinegar, wine vinegars). Seasoned rice vinegar is vinegar that has sugar and salt added to it, and all by itself it is a fabulous fat-free salad dressing. You can also add to it: crushed garlic, mustard, capers, soy sauce/Bragg's Liquid Aminos. Try a new kind of vinegar every month.
3. Dried herbs and spices: cumin, coriander, sage, marjoram, basil, oregano, thyme, dill, dried mustard, paprika, cayenne pepper, hot pepper flakes, black pepper, salt, garlic powder. Buy them as new recipes call for them, and save money by buying them in the bulk section of a natural foods store.
4. Mustard.
5. Vegetable broth powder or canned vegetable broth.
6. Nut and seed butters; nuts and seeds (sesame, sunflower, pumpkin).
7. Dried beans and legumes. Canned or dried black or red beans, garbanzo, kidney, pinto, lentils, plus red lentils, split peas, limas.
8. Grains such as barley, bulgur, couscous, millet, rolled oats, quick oats, and/or instant oatmeal, polenta, popcorn, quinoa, brown rice, wheat berries, wheat germ; whole grain Italian pasta (macaroni, spaghetti, etc), ready-to-eat whole cereal.
9. Breads: Whole wheat bread, whole wheat pita, rice cakes, flour and corn tortillas, or chapattis.

10. Fresh and frozen fruit; lemons or limes; dried fruits (apples, apricots, currants, dates, figs, papaya, peaches, raisins).
11. Canned tomato products: diced, stewed, sauce, paste; spaghetti sauce; vegetarian baked beans.
12. Soy products: tofu (in aseptic boxes), tempeh, miso (fermented soybean paste has a salty taste and can be used in place of Parmesan cheese in pesto); textured vegetable protein (TVP).
13. Prepared foods: Instant dried bean mixes (black beans, refried beans).
14. Fortified soymilk, rice milk, or oat milk.
15. Fats: olive oil, flaxseed oil, and canola oil.

Ten Delicious Alternatives to Cow's Milk

(Not to be used as a substitute for human mother's milk or infant formula)

❂

1. Soymilk.
2. Rice milk.
3. Almond milk.
4. Oat milk.
5. Hemp milk.
6. Chocolate soymilk.
7. Enriched soymilk (Vitamin D, B_{12}, Omega-3 added).
8. Smoothie made of any of the above plus frozen banana and berries.
9. Chai tea made with any one of 1 to 7 above.
10. Hot chocolate made with any one of 1 to 7 above.

Ten Tips for Supermarket Shopping

1. Eat something before you go food shopping. A banana or a sandwich will work—anything to keep you from being hungry in the store. It is too easy to buy on impulse when shopping on an empty stomach.

2. If you wear reading glasses, bring them. It's important to read ingredients on labels.

3. Bring a shopping list. (Check your pantry to see what needs to be replaced and prepare the list based on that and recipes you want to follow.)

4. Visit the outer aisles first. Produce is usually along an outer wall. This is where you'll find the most bang for your buck and the best ratio of nutrients to calories.

5. Try to make your basket as colorful as possible. Look for bright colors and fruits and vegetables that are in season. Color is where the antioxidants are. Be sure to buy enough fruit to snack on throughout the day, and dark leafy green vegetables for a portion or two per person for every day.

6. Buy organic whenever possible. Ask for organic fruits and vegetables if you don't see them. (Strawberries, raisins, grapes, and peanuts for peanut butter are grown with the most chemicals, so encourage the store manager to find organic sources of these foods.)

7. Read labels on all packaged foods. Avoid products with long lists of ingredients. Avoid anything with hydrogenated or partially hydrogenated oils.

8. The fewer ingredients the better. Avoid foods with ingredients you cannot pronounce, especially those that sound like something that was made in chemistry class.

9. The first ingredient in bread, crackers, or cereals should be "whole" or "sprouted" whether it's whole or sprouted wheat, rye, spelt, or any other grain. Don't be fooled by the word "unbleached."

10. Save money by buying grains, legumes, and spices in bulk. Some stores even sell oatmeal and other cereals in bulk bins.

Ten Tips for Eating in Restaurants

1. Before you go, look for a vegetarian friendly restaurant on www.HappyCow.net or www.VegDining.com. If you can't find one, try to choose an ethnic restaurant where there will be vegetarian options on the menu. Chinese, Japanese, Thai, Italian, Indian, Mexican, and other foreign cuisines offer many good choices without meat.

2. If there are no vegetarian entrées, you can try to determine if a meat meal can be prepared without the meat. Pasta can be made with vegetables instead of meatballs. Meat can be left off any sandwich. Grilled mushrooms are terrific without the hamburger. And a meal can be made with the foods that accompany a meat item on the menu (potatoes, lentils, grilled vegetables, etc.). If you are too shy to ask for what you want, try joining a local Toastmasters group and learn to speak up comfortably.

3. Even in a deli, you can order a Reuben sandwich with sauerkraut and avocado instead of the meat. You will be surprised at how tasty this can be on rye bread.

4. Pasta with steamed, roasted, or grilled vegetables in an olive oil–garlic sauce is good. And most restaurants offer salads to accompany the most simple pasta dish.

5. Don't be afraid to ask for the side dishes. Combine a set of side dishes and/or appetizers into your own specialized vegetable plate.

6. If necessary, a baked potato topped with ingredients from the salad bar can make a filling and delicious meal.

7. When ordering in restaurants, ask for broccoli or bok choy to be added to your dish. Even if they are not part of the item you order, they can be added to many dishes, especially in Chinese and Italian restaurants.

8. When eating at a salad bar, avoid the prepared dressings and salads made with mayonnaise. Choose vegetables, nuts, and seeds over heavily dressed premixed salads.

9. Use balsamic vinegar or a little olive oil or let the wetter vegetables (beets, peas, corn) "dress" the salad. Or ask for fresh lemon to squeeze on your food.

10. Instead of a cheese and pepperoni pizza: order a pizza with tomato sauce, lots of veggies, garlic, onions, olives, and any other vegetarian topping. Carol likes to dribble some red wine vinegar and olive oil over it.

Ten Foods to Eat When There's "Nothing in The House"

1. Chickpeas from a can, heated in the toaster oven.
2. Spaghetti with olive oil and garlic.
3. Peanut butter sandwich.
4. Fresh fruit.
5. Canned pineapple.
6. Jam on crackers.
7. Carrots (baby carrots) or celery.
8. Raisins or other dried fruits.
9. Popcorn (in bulk, organic; add nutritional yeast, oregano, Bragg's Liquid Aminos to it).
10. Toasted sesame, sunflower, or pumpkin seeds in a bowl.

Ten Tips for Using Toasted Sesame Seeds

1. Throw them on a salad.
2. Sprinkle them on steamed vegetables.
3. Add to a nut loaf.
4. Add them to cabbage salad.
5. Snack on them in a bowl.
6. Substitute for sesame oil in recipes (grind in a coffee grinder first).
7. Add to soup or sauces.
8. Sprinkle on popcorn.
9. Dip tofu in tamari mixed with orange juice and then in the seeds. Bake.
10. Sprinkle in with the contents of a wrap.

Ten Ways to Increase the Colors of Your Food

1. Blue-purple (fresh): Add blackberries, blueberries, raisins to your cereal.
2. Blue-purple (fresh): snack on purple grapes, dried plums.
3. Blue-purple (cooked): Slice eggplant and grill or roast with a little olive oil.
4. Green (fresh): Keep a fruit bowl in the kitchen with green apples, kiwi fruit, green grapes, or pears.
5. Green (fresh): Include celery, romaine lettuce, spinach in your salads.
6. Green (cooked): Include broccoli, green beans, cabbage, and peas in your stir-fries and soups.
7. White (cooked): Learn Indian dishes that use cauliflower, onions, potatoes, garlic, and mushrooms.
8. Red (fresh): Snack on red apples, tomatoes, cherries, red grapefruit, red pears, strawberries, watermelon, radishes, red grapes, and raspberries.
9. Red (fresh or cooked): Include cranberries, beets, red onions, or red potatoes in your dinner.
10. Yellow-orange (fresh or cooked): Include cantaloupe, bananas, brown pears, lemons, grapefruit, yellow apples, oranges, mangoes, peaches, tangerines, carrots, pumpkins, corn, sweet potatoes, and squash throughout the year.

Ten Things to Do with Flax Seeds

1. Grind flax seeds in a coffee grinder and keep the ground seeds in the freezer.
2. Sprinkle them on salads.
3. Add them to pancake and waffle batter.
4. Sprinkle them on cereal.
5. Include them in smoothies.
6. Add to all baked goods recipes.
7. Dip tofu in tamari with orange juice or pomegranate juice and coat in flax seeds mixed with wheat germ. Bake.
8. Dehydrate them and make "raw" crackers.
9. Add to nut loaf or veggie burger recipes.
10. Add water to ground flax seeds to make a paste that substitutes for eggs in baked goods.

Ten Comfort Foods

1. Mashed potatoes and gravy (see page 144).
2. Mac Daddy (see page 109).
3. BLT's: vegetarian bacon, lettuce, and tomato sandwiches. "Smart Bacon" is Patti's favorite brand; she microwaves six slices for two minutes and 10 seconds).
4. Hot chocolate made with soymilk. (You could use "AhLaska" or powdered chocolate mix like Ghiradelli's double chocolate mix.)
5. Orzo pilaf (it's creamy, and with the additional sautéed mushrooms rich and warming!) (see page 103).
6. Toast and jam, especially chocolate bread with raspberry jam (see page 117).
7. Imagine Creamy Portobello Mushroom Soup with grilled diced Portobello mushrooms and a little sherry added to it.
8. Scones and soymilk (see page 112).
9. Potato pancakes (see page 107).
10. Matzoh ball soup (see page 66).

AND: Any food you remember your mother or grandmother making. (Google the food with the word "vegan" in front of it, and you will probably be able to reproduce it without the animal ingredients).

Ten Things to Do with Nutritional Yeast

1. Sprinkle on salads.
2. Sprinkle on popcorn.
3. Sprinkle on any pasta dish.
4. Add to certain soups (for instance, Cheddary Cheez Soup, page 64).
5. Make Mac Daddy (Macaroni and cheese) (see page 109).
6. Use in marinade for tofu.
7. Sprinkle on roasted or steamed vegetables.
8. Sprinkle on baked potatoes.
9. Add to polenta.
10. Use in scrambled tofu (see page 47).

Ten Scrumptious Frozen Dairy-Free Desserts

1. Rice Dream.
2. Soy Delicious.
3. Purely Decadent.
4. Temptation (Carol's favorite).
5. Coconut Bliss.
6. Tofutti Cuties (sandwiches).
7. Soy Delicious (sandwiches).
8. Soy Dream Lil' Dreamers (sandwiches).
9. Most sorbets (not sherbet which is made with dairy, but sorbet which is made without dairy).
10. Frozen bananas through the Champion juicer.

Part Two

How to Cook like a Vegetarian

Plant-based recipes are all-forgiving. This isn't French cuisine. If you are just cooking for yourself and your family, and you don't have the ingredient, you can substitute something else. This is the way our grandmothers cooked. They would add a little of this or a little of that. After cooking the suggested ways of preparing certain foods two or three times, you will be able to decide for yourself, "Do I do this with a little of this, or a lot of this?"

If you are able to commit to learning just two main course dishes that you like, you will be able to eat like a vegetarian! With a variety of soups, salads, dips, and side dishes, you will be able to feed yourself, your family, and your guests with a wide variety of creative and nourishing menus.

Learning the Tricks, Hints, and Shortcuts for Cooking

W ho has time to cook? This busy lifestyle and time crunch are often what scare people from trying to eat like a vegetarian. We hope this book shows you how to save plenty of time. But even when a meal takes a few minutes to prepare, a change in perspective can help you find more time even while food is cooking.

It may be hard to imagine a time when cooking will provide an escape from the busy life that is keeping you from cooking! Or that the rhythmic action of cooking can become a form of meditation or prayer. Or that cooking awakens all of your senses—the sound of the vegetables being chopped, the smell of spices and fresh herbs, roasted veggies, or fresh fruit, the sight of a beautiful salad, or simply of a peach in all its ripeness, and then of course, the taste and textures of the great food. Cooking can bring you to your senses!

But you aren't there yet, you might protest, and you might not want to be. *You want to eat like a vegetarian*, you might be thinking, *not cook like a New Ager*.

People who go from never, never cooking to sometimes cooking require recipes. It's like when a baby learns to walk, she requires a table to hold onto, a couch to reach for. A recipe is like the table; it helps you get your footing. But once you discover how delicious the food is, and how creative you can be with a plant-based diet and this new way of eating, then you can run off in every direction, like a toddler.

We hope that by this point you have discovered the possibility of eating like a vegetarian without following a recipe. The first time you follow a recipe you should probably do it as close to possible as it is written. But, after this, you can make it your own by fiddling with it—this helps build your confidence and tailors the recipe to your taste.

We want to say something in favor of cooking. For a small investment of time in preparing food, which nourishes us physically, we can nourish ourselves in countless other ways, too.

Think of the gratitude you feel if someone cooks a meal for you. When somebody takes the time to prepare food for us, it is one of the greatest gifts in this hurried world. And we can give ourselves this gift every day.

People who don't cook rob themselves of "down time." Cooking, surprisingly, provides opportunities to do some things that we think we don't have time to do. Even though a dish may take 15 minutes to prepare, once it's in the oven or on the stove, the cook then has a half hour or more either to do yoga, or meditate, or call his mom, or balance her checkbook, or do any one of the hundreds of things we all wish we had more time to do.

If you are eating out in a restaurant and the whole meal takes forty-five minutes, or you are picking up prepared food to bring home to eat, there is no down time in the entire process. There is no time to replenish yourself, to take a breath, to take care of the small things that determine whether we feel rushed and out of breath or nourished and calm. It is the act of preparing food for ourselves and those we love, as much as the food itself, that nourishes us.

If you are afraid to cook or think you don't have time to cook or have never cooked or don't have confidence in the kitchen, this is the chapter for you. Basically, in this chapter, we are going to share the tricks and the hints and the shortcuts, so that cooking food will be like popping a tape in the VCR. Notice we didn't say, *programming* the VCR.

If you wanted to learn how to drive, you would take a driving class, not a class on understanding the internal combustion engine. Some people who want to learn to cook sign up for a gourmet vegetarian cooking class and then conclude that vegetarian cooking takes too long. In reality, all they have to do is steam some veggies and prepare some whole grains. Food that is simple to prepare is just as nourishing and delicious as fancy food, and takes one-tenth the time.

We aren't inviting you to go for a PhD in vegan cuisine, we're inviting you out to the playground! Get your hands wet, learn your way around the kitchen, and have something delicious and fun at mealtime and snack time.

The recipes in this book are elastic; you can stretch them and shape them and personalize them. You can make them your own.

Sometimes the difference between an easy recipe and a hard recipe is whether or not you've made it before and whether or not you have all the ingredients on hand without having to shop.

And remember this: When you have an ingredient you want to showcase, especially fruit, instead of searching for a recipe that highlights it, just serve it. If you have an exquisite bunch of grapes, rather than find a recipe to show them off, serve them on a platter. You can do the same with tangerines or pears. Sometimes it's nice to let the fruit be fruit.

Ten Tips for Effortless Meals

1. Before you unpack the groceries or check your email or go the bathroom, put the water on to boil. Whether you are basing your meal on pasta, potato, or grains, you will want boiling water to cook the food at the center of the plate.

2. After buying fresh produce, prepare it when you get home. Store ready to use foods in airtight containers.

3. Create your own salad bar. From chickpeas to sliced carrots, sprouts to shredded cabbage, have an assortment of colorful and healthy choices ready to toss into a salad.

4. Get a blender, a food processor, and a chef's knife—that's all you need. (A juicer is nice but not necessary.)

5. Pita (pocket bread) makes sandwiches easy. Always put the cut or torn-off piece of bread in the pocket first. Then fill it with hummus or mashed or instant beans. Try adding dark greens, tomatoes, and sprouts.

6. Tortillas—roll up leftovers in tortillas and create instant meals. You can spread salsa, mustard, eggless mayo, hoisin, hummus, or any other sauce on the tortilla first if you like.

7. Canned fruit, especially in the winter and packed in its own juice, is a great addition to salads or desserts.

8. Use frozen veggies often and keep some in the freezer at all times. They are just as nutritious as fresh.

9. Keep seasoned rice vinegar on hand as an all-purpose salad dressing.

10. Instant Pita pizza or English muffin pizza: Take a pita pocket or an opened English muffin; swirl some tomato sauce on top; sprinkle with nutritional yeast; add veggies/spinach/artichoke hearts. Warm in a toaster oven.

Starting with Breakfasts

Many people, vegetarian or not, eat the same breakfast every day. While variety is nice, reality is more compelling, and most of us are rushed in the morning.

A healthy breakfast can be delicious and sweet and still take no more time to prepare than it takes to stop at a coffee shop and shout an order over the counter. Cookbooks with long sections on breakfast make things harder than they have to be. Sure, once in a while it's nice to be able to make pancakes or waffles. But most of the time, most of us eat a simple breakfast every day. These days, Patti's breakfast is usually a bowl of cereal (or a bowl of rice or millet left over from dinner) with soymilk and fruit, flax seeds, and walnuts on top. On cold days it's hot cereal. If she's in a big hurry, she skips the cereal part and just eats the fruit with flax seeds and walnuts. And sometimes she tosses the fruit, seeds, and some juice into the blender with a banana to make a fruit smoothie. Carol loves to have granola with fresh pineapple or bananas.

When eating breakfast out we usually eat hot oatmeal and half a grapefruit, or a bagel or whole wheat toast with jam.

Besides having soymilk over cereal, you can also add to the cereal:

- About 1/2 cup assorted frozen berries (microwave to defrost)
- About 1 tablespoon ground flax seeds
- About 1 tablespoon walnuts (approximately 3 to 5 walnut halves).

SMOOTHIES

Smoothies, an irresistible combination of frozen fruit with liquid, are quick, soothing, healthy, nourishing, and fun to make. A variety of smoothies can be created from a basic understanding of how they work and what is at the core of their existence: frozen bananas. Freeze bananas before they turn completely limp and brown. Freeze them by peeling them, cutting them into chunks about 2 inches long, and keeping them in plastic bags. Then it's simply a matter of 1, 2, 3.

1. Frozen bananas (If you forgot to freeze the bananas, unfrozen bananas work well, too. The smoothie won't be as frothy or cold, but it will still be as delicious.)

   plus

2. Liquid: soymilk or rice milk or juices (singly or a combination): apple/orange/pineapple, straight or diluted with water

   plus

3. Frozen or fresh fruit: strawberries, mangoes, raspberries, blueberries, pineapple, or any other fruit

Optional:
You can add 1/2 cup of silken tofu for more protein; and/or ice; and/or sweetener (including jam).

Examples:
- Frozen bananas, soymilk, a couple of tablespoons raspberry jam
- Frozen bananas, orange juice, soymilk, silken tofu, a little vanilla
- Frozen bananas, pineapple-coconut juice, frozen blueberries

- Frozen bananas, mangoes, soymilk, a little sweetener
- Frozen bananas, papaya juice, peaches
- Frozen bananas, strawberries, soymilk
- Frozen bananas, strawberries, apple juice

- Place all ingredients into the blender and process on high speed.
- Stop and check to make sure all the fruit has been blended up; dip a spatula into the mixture to help the fruit move to the center. Then blend again. The smoothie will be smooth and thick.

A Sample Smoothie

About half a cup of organically grown blueberries
1 banana
About 10 ounces of orange juice
1 Bosc pear, cut into eighths
1 gala apple, cut into eighths
About a tablespoon of ground flax seeds

- Buzz the blender for about a full minute.

Frozen berries: When fresh berries are not available, organic frozen mixed berries are desirable. And when the store is out of those, we buy frozen blueberries or frozen raspberries or frozen black berries, or all three and mix them ourselves.

Serves 1 or 2

EASY FRENCH TOAST

2 ripe bananas
1 cup fortified soymilk
8 slices bread
Olive oil or canola oil
Optional: cinammon or nutmeg

- In a blender, blend the bananas and soymilk until completely smooth.
- Pour into a large bowl.
- Dip the pieces of bread into the banana mixture and fry in a lightly oiled, non-stick pan until browned on both sides.

Serves 4

LUSCIOUS OATMEAL

The only thing you need to know for making oatmeal is to boil slightly more than twice as much water as the amount of oatmeal you are going to cook:

1 cup of oatmeal = two 1/4 cups of water

2 cups of oatmeal = four 1⁄2 cups of water

- Put water and oatmeal mixture in pot and bring to a boil.
- As the water comes to a boil, cut up some fresh fruit—an apple, a pear, a banana, a peach—if you want to add color and more flavor to the oatmeal.
- When the water has come to a boil, add any dried fruit you want to add (dried cherries, raisins, dates, cranberries).
- Add nutmeg and cinnamon if you wish.
- Turn down the heat to simmer, and stir for about five minutes.
- Remove from heat, add some soymilk if you wish, and let rest for five minutes.
- Top with fresh cut fruit, dried fruit, flax seeds, and some walnuts if you wish.

SCRAMBLED TOFU

1 tablespoon olive oil
3 garlic cloves, minced
8 to 10 medium mushrooms, sliced
1/2 cup grated carrots
1/2 cup chopped scallion
1/4 teaspoon turmeric
3 tablespoons nutritional yeast
1 pound regular firm tofu, crumbled
1 tablespoon soy sauce
1 cup spinach leaves

- Heat the oil over medium-high heat, then sauté the mushrooms and garlic until they are golden on one side.
- When you flip the mushrooms and garlic over, add the carrots and scallion. Sauté them together for about 2 minutes.
- Add the tofu, nutritional yeast flakes, turmeric, and soy sauce. Stir them together, and continue cooking for about 5 minutes.
- Add spinach, and let it cook for about one minute. It will become slightly wilted but still hold its shape.
- Serve and enjoy.

If you don't have all of the veggies, you can leave them out or add your favorites.

Serves 4

Soy "Butter"milk Biscuits

These are absolutely the best biscuits. They go great with jam.

A scant 1 tablespoon apple cider vinegar
3/4 cup soymilk
1 cup white flour
1 1/2 cup spelt or whole wheat pastry flour
1/4 teaspoon baking soda
1/2 teaspoon salt
1/3 cup light olive oil

- Preheat the oven to 450°F.
- Measure the apple cider vinegar and place into a measuring cup. Pour the soymilk in until it measures 3/4 cup. Leave to curdle while combining the dry ingredients.
- Sift together the flours, baking powder, baking soda, and salt into a mixing bowl.
- Make a well in the center, and pour in the oil and soy "butter" milk. Use a fork to combine until mixed. But do not overmix the biscuits. Mix quickly and conservatively.
- Lightly flour a surface, and turn the dough onto it. Knead it gently a few times. Pat the dough so that it is about 1/2 inch thick. Using a biscuit cutter or a glass, cut the dough into 10 to 12 biscuits.
- Place them so that they touch each other on an ungreased baking sheet.
- Bake for 10 to 12 minutes, until golden brown. Serve immediately.

Makes 10 to 12 biscuits

Salads

●

AZTEC SALAD

This salad is a fiesta of color and taste. It may be made in advance, and keeps well for several days. If you are one of those folks who dislikes cilantro, simply omit it. If you are a cilantro-lover, you may want to double the amount.

Let sit overnight and flavors meld.

1 1/2 cups dry black beans—OR—3 15-ounce cans black beans
3 1/2 cups water
2 cups frozen corn, thawed
2 large tomatoes, diced
1 large green bell pepper, diced
1 large red or yellow bell pepper, diced
1/2 cup chopped red onion
1/2 cup chopped fresh cilantro
2 tablespoons seasoned rice vinegar
2 tablespoons apple cider or distilled vinegar
1 lime or lemon, juiced
2 garlic cloves, minced
2 teaspoons cumin
1 teaspoon coriander
1/4 teaspoon crushed red pepper—OR—a pinch of cayenne
1/2 to 1 teaspoon salt

- Sort through beans to remove any debris, then wash them and place them in a large pan or bowl with 6 cups of water. Soak overnight. Pour off soaking water and place in a kettle with 3 1/2 cups of fresh water. Bring to a simmer, and cook until tender. This should take 45 minutes to an hour. Do not overcook the beans or they will be mushy and unattractive in the salad. Drain and cool the cooked beans. If you are using canned black beans, simply drain them and proceed.
- When the beans are cool, combine them with the corn, tomatoes, bell peppers, red onion, and fresh cilantro.
- Whisk together dressing ingredients and pour over the salad. Toss gently to mix.

Serves 10

From *The Peaceful Palate* by Jennifer Raymond. Used with permission.

CHOPPED VEGETABLE SALAD

Patti's mother inspired this recipe. She often prepares a salad of thinly sliced cucumbers (peeled first) marinated with onions in lots of seasoned rice vinegar and lots of black pepper. Patti borrowed her pepper and rice vinegar dressing and changed her recipe as follows, for a chopped vegetable salad that tastes even better on days two and three after it's been marinating for a while.

1 can garbanzo beans, drained
3 to 6 large red radishes, sliced
3 stalks celery, chopped
2 large carrots, peeled and chopped
2 inch section of daikon radish, chopped (optional)
2 large leaves of collard greens, stems removed and chopped (optional)
3 to 4 green onions, chopped (optional)
1/4 to 1/2 cup seasoned rice vinegar
1/4 teaspoon ground black pepper, or more to taste

● Mix all ingredients in a bowl

Serves 8

POTATO SALAD

4 large or 20 small potatoes cut into 2-inch chunks
4 tablespoons capers, with liquid from jar of capers
3 stalks celery, chopped
2 carrots, sliced in half and then into half circles
Optional: 3 tablespoons Dijon mustard

- Steam potatoes for about 10 minutes.
- Mix steamed potatoes and all other ingredients.

- Potato Salad variations
  - Add olives and/or chopped parsley.
  - Omit the capers, and instead add chopped mushrooms (1/2 pound), 1 chopped fennel bulb, 1/4 cup lemon juice, and a small amount of olive oil.
  - Use roasted potatoes instead of steamed potatoes.
  - Add 1/2 cup artichoke hearts and sun-dried red tomatoes (reconstituted), with some fresh dill or basil.
- Optional: If you don't want the crunch, you can steam the carrots and celery along with the potatoes. Also, for color, you can add fresh or frozen corn, fresh or frozen peas, zucchini, fennel, and/or any other veggies you have in the house.

Serves 4 to 6

Quinoa Salad

Carol's friend Tiina fixed this for a large family celebration—every person there loved it. Don't be limited by our suggestions for veggies: you can add avocado, fresh corn, red onion, cilantro, or olives.

1 cup quinoa
2 cups water
1/2 cup each of a variety of vegetables: choose from asparagus, steamed carrot, celery, cucumber, tomato, broccoli, and red pepper
1/2 cup toasted sunflower seeds

Dressing:
1/4 cup olive oil
1/4 cup lemon juice or rice vinegar
2 cloves garlic
1 tablespoon tamari
1/2 teaspoon of basil and oregano

- Rinse quinoa. This is important because its natural coating can be rather bitter.
- Bring water to a boil, stir the quinoa in, cover, reduce heat and cook for 10 to 15 minutes. Cook until all the water is absorbed.
- Cool the quinoa.
- Combine vegetables, cooked quinoa, and dressing. Stir.
- Serve on a bed of lettuce and garnish with lemon wedges.

Serves 4

Lentil Salad

This is a great summer salad.

Salad
1 1/2 cups lentils
1 cup chopped onions
2 garlic cloves, chopped
4 cups water
1 cup finely chopped red or green bell peppers
1 cup finely chopped celery
1 cup finely chopped red onions

Curried mango tofu dressing
1 12-ounce box of soft silken tofu
1 tablespoon fresh lime juice
4 tablespoons prepared mango chutney
2 teaspoons curry powder
2 teaspoons finely minced red onions

- Combine the lentils, onions, garlic and water in a large saucepan. Bring the ingredients to a boil, reduce the heat, and simmer for 30 to 40 minutes. The lentils should be tender, but don't cook them too long because they will become mushy. Some people simmer for only 15 to 20 minutes to keep the lentils crunchy.
- Using a nonmetal bowl, combine the peppers, celery, and onions.
- When the lentils are tender, drain them, and, while still warm, place

them in the bowl. Stir them together with the raw vegetables. Set the bowl aside for 15 minutes.

- In a blender, blend the tofu and lime juice. Empty into a bowl, stir in the chutney, curry powder, and red onions.
- Stir the dressing into the lentil-vegetable mixture. Serve.

Serves 4 to 6

- Lentil salad variations: Instead of the curry dressing:
  - Mix together 2 tablespoons olive oil, a minced clove of garlic, 1 lemon juiced, 1/4 teaspoon of thyme and cumin. Pour this onto the lentil mixture.
  - Or use 1 tablespoon capers instead of the cumin and add 1/4 cup of minced chives
  - Or use 2 tangerines instead of lemon. Juice one tangerine and peel and chop the other one (making sure not to get any of the seeds). Add to the lentils.
  - Or add a tomato, a few radishes, a small carrot to the salad and use as a salad dressing: 2 tablespoons olive oil, a tablespoon each of balsamic vinegar and lemon juice, 1 tablespoon Dijon mustard, and 1 clove garlic.
  - Or use 4 tablespoons olive oil, 4 tablespoons red vinegar, 1 clove garlic, 2 tablespoons capers as the dressing, and add 3 tablespoons chopped dill pickles, 6 tablespoons chopped parsley, 2 tablespoons chopped fresh chives and tarragon (each). Mix together and let rest for 1 to 2 hours.

Soups

A few quick summer soups.

Carrot Avocado Soup

2 cups of carrot juice
1 whole avocado
1 to 2 teaspoons ginger, grated
Dulse seaweed (optional)

- Blend the juice, avocado, and ginger in a blender.
- Top with a sprinkle of dulse.

Serves 2

Tomato-horseradish Soup

5 ripe tomatoes, chopped and with seeds removed
1/2 teaspoon horseradish
1 tablespoon diced onion
lemon juice
black pepper to taste

- Mix, refrigerate, serve in shallow bowls or goblets and enjoy.

MELON SOUP

2 ripe small cantaloupes or 1 cantaloupe and one honeydew melon
1 lime, juiced
1 1/2 cups water

Optional: 2 kiwis, peeled and thinly sliced and 1/2 pint raspberries

- Cut the melons in half, remove the seeds, and then remove the "meat" from the melons. Chop melon pieces into large cubes.
- Put half of each melon into the food processor with 1/2 of the lime juice and 3/4 cup water. Pulse it. Empty processor and repeat.
- Mix the puréed melon soup together and serve in bowls.
- Garnish each soup bowl with kiwi and raspberries, if desired.

Red Gazpacho

You can use fresh tomatoes in the body of the soup if you wish, but using canned tomatoes makes this a very quick recipe to prepare. Make it in the morning and keep in the refrigerator until lunch or dinner so that the tastes can meld.

1 28-ounce canned tomatoes
1/2 cup water
2 teaspoon "chicken flavor" vegetable stock
1/4 cup vinegar
4 tablespoons olive oil
Handful of parsley
6 to 8 basil springs
3 to 4 cloves garlic
1 small onion, peeled and quartered
1 green pepper, seeded and quartered
1 cucumber, peeled
Pepper to taste
Handful of cherry tomatoes
4 scallions
Croutons
Dash of Tabasco

- Prepare the vegetables. To prepare the cucumber, slice it in half lengthwise, and deseed. Then slice each half in half, lengthwise. Reserve one quarter of the green pepper and of the cucumber.
- Bring the water to a boil, and add the vegetable stock to it.

- Empty the canned tomatoes into a blender or food processor. Add the olive oil, parsley, basil, and garlic, stock, and vinegar. Purée it.
- Empty three-quarters of the mixture into a container, then add the green pepper, the onion, and the cucumber to the food processor. Pulse briefly, so that the vegetables remain chewy. You may need to do this in two batches, so that the ingredients fit and don't become over processed. Mix the processed veggies with the puréed tomatoes and flavoring. Add a dash of Tabasco.
- Refrigerate for several hours, so that the flavors influence each other.
- Before serving, dice the scallions, the reserved green pepper, and cucumber. Chop the tomatoes. Place each vegetable into its own small bowl (Carol uses oriental tea cups), and put the croutons in a larger bowl.
- Taste the soup and adjust the seasonings. It should taste lively. It may need more pepper and salt. Carol mixes an additional tablespoon of olive oil in that this time.
- Serve in bowls, letting each guest add the finely minced veggies to their soup bowls.

Serves 4 heartily

GREEN GAZPACHO

4 large cucumbers, peeled and seeds removed, chopped in large pieces

2 ripe avocados, halved, pitted, and scooped out

3 medium garlic cloves

2 medium green bell peppers, seeds and ribs removed, chopped in large pieces

4 green onions, chopped in large pieces

2 cups water

Juice of 1 1/2 lemons

1/3 small bunch of cilantro, cleaned

Freshly ground black pepper

Pinch of cayenne pepper

Paprika

Water as needed

- Set aside a few sprigs of the cilantro for garnish.
- Put cucumber, avocado, garlic, peppers, and onions in food processor.
- Blend until creamy, adding water a little at a time to desired consistency.
- Add lemon juice, cilantro, salt, pepper, and cayenne to taste.
- Serve with paprika sprinkled on top and cilantro for garnish.
- (If using a blender, rather than a food processor, add the cucumbers slowly at first, blending as you go, so there's a liquid base for the other ingredients.)

Serves 4 to 6

MISO SOUP

Miso should never be added to boiling water, but to water that has just stopped boiling. One way to add miso to make soup, is to remove about 1/2 cup of hot water into a cup, add the miso to the water in the cup, stir until dissolved, then add this mixture back to the soup pot. As you become familiar and comfortable with miso you can mix two flavors together (chickpea and red miso for instance, or white miso with red).

3 cups water
3 to 4 tablespoons miso
1 green onion, chopped
Any other chopped vegetable such as carrot, celery, mushroom, cauli-
    flower, etc. (optional)

- Bring water to a boil.
- Add onion and any vegetables.
- Let them simmer in the water for about five minutes.
- Mix miso with about 1/2 cup of water.
- Return to soup pot.
- Optional: add a few cubes of diced silken tofu.

Serves 4 to 5

Cabbage and Chickpea Soup

Using canned organic tomatoes makes the preparation even faster. Two cups of chopped cabbage is less than one quarter of a large head, so any leftover chunks of cabbage are perfect for this. (Green cabbage makes a prettier soup, but we've made it with red cabbage, and that works well too.) And once, when Patti was out of fresh parsley, she made it with dried parsley and it was only minutely different. So here's the recipe, with Patti's comments in parenthesis. We hope you like it as much as we do.

2 teaspoons olive oil or canola oil (or less)
1 onion chopped
1 clove garlic, crushed or minced
1 teaspoon paprika
1 cup chopped tomato, fresh or canned
2 cups chopped cabbage
1 potato, diced (peel potato first if using a Russet potato)
1/4 cup finely chopped fresh parsley
4 cups water or vegetable stock (I've only made it with water.)
1 15-ounce can garbanzo beans, drained and rinsed
1/4 teaspoon black pepper
1/2 to 1 teaspoon salt

- Heat the oil in a large pot and sauté the onion until it is soft, about 3 to 5 minutes.
- Add the garlic, chopped tomato, cabbage, potato, parsley, water or stock, garbanzo beans, paprika, and black pepper.

- Simmer until the potato and cabbage are tender, about 15 minutes.
- Ladle approximately 3 cups of the soup into a blender. Blend until smooth, being sure to hold the lid on tightly and start on low speed.
- Return the blended soup to the pot and stir to mix, adding salt to taste.

Serves 4 to 6

From *The Peaceful Palate* by Jennifer Raymond. Used with permission.

CHEDDARY CHEEZ SOUP

Meat eaters and vegetarians can't believe this is vegan. It is a delicious soup or can be used as a dip for breads and vegetables.

1 medium potato, peeled and coarsely chopped
1 medium carrot, peeled and coarsely chopped
1 medium onion, peeled and coarsely chopped
1 cup water
1 package Lite Silken Tofu (firm) crumbled
1/2 cup nutritional yeast
2 tablespoons fresh lemon juice
1 1/4 teaspoons salt
1 teaspoon onion granules
1/4 teaspoon garlic granules
1 cup low-fat, regular nondairy milk

- Place the potato, carrot, onion, and water in a 2-quart saucepan, and bring to a boil. Reduce the heat to medium, cover the saucepan with a lid, and simmer the vegetables, stirring once or twice, for 10 minutes or until they are tender.
- Purée the soup in batches. To do this, transfer a small portion of the cooked vegetables, some of the cooking water, and a small amount of each of the remaining ingredients *except the milk* to a blender.
- Process each batch until the mixture is completely smooth. Pour the blended soup into a large mixing bowl.
- Continue processing the rest of the vegetables, the cooking water, and

the remaining ingredients in a similar fashion, adding them to the mixing bowl as they are blended.

- Return the blended soup to the saucepan, and stir in the milk.
- Place the saucepan over low heat, and warm the soup through, stirring often, until it is hot.

- Variations: Prepare the recipe as directed above. Then add one of the following options to the finished soup:

  - Broccoli Cheez Soup or Cauliflower Cheez Soup: Add 1 1/2 cups broccoli or cauliflower, cut or broken into small florets, and steamed until tender.

  - Cheezy Vegetable Soup: Add 1 10-ounce package of frozen vegetables, cooked according to the package directions, and drained.

  - Green Peas and Cheez Soup: Add 1 1/2 cups frozen, loose-pack green peas, cooked according to the package directions, and drained.

  - Herbed Cheddary Cheez Soup: Add 1 to 1 1/2 teaspoons of your favorite dried herb or 4 teaspoons of your favorite chopped fresh herb. Herbs may also be added to the other variations above. Dill weed is particularly nice with green peas. Thyme or oregano is a good match with mixed vegetables. Basil is a pleasant complement to broccoli.

Serves 4

From *Vegan Vittles* by Jo Stepaniak. Used with permission.

Matzoh Ball Soup

12 cups vegetable broth. (Patti likes Seitenbacher vegetable broth powder, one teaspoon per cup of water; but any good broth will do.)
3 carrots, thinly sliced
1 cup cauliflower florets, chopped very small
matzoh balls (see next page)

- Bring broth to a low boil and add the vegetables and matzoh balls.
- Cook for 10 minutes and serve.

Serves 5

Thanks to Regina Heitner for suggesting the vegetables. They add a wonderful dimension to the matzoh ball soup!

Matzoh Balls

These can be made in advance and stored in a covered bowl with some soup stock or water in it. It helps to separate the balls and rotate which ones are in the liquid if you store them for more than a day before serving.

This recipe makes 15 smallish matzoh balls. Patti usually plans for three balls per person, but you can plan on two per person and make them bigger.

Matzoh ball soup is traditionally served at Passover, though many people enjoy it year round. Patti and her sister have happy memories of giggling fits from years when their grandmother would always ask loudly at the Passover table, "How did my balls come out this year?" These vegetarian balls always come out delicious.

Large pot with about 12 cups water.
6 tablespoons olive oil
3 tablespoons Ener-G Egg Replacer* and 1/2 cup water
1 1/2 cups matzoh meal
6+ tablespoons vegetable soup stock
1 teaspoon salt

- Bring pot of water to a low boil.
- In a blender, blend egg replacer and 1/2 cup water. Blend until frothy (a second or two).
- Add oil and blend another second or two.
- In a bowl, combine matzoh meal and salt.
- Pour blender mixture into the bowl with the matzoh meal and salt.

Mix well with your hands adding the soup stock as needed to make a thick batter.

- Refrigerate the batter in a covered bowl for at least twenty minutes.
- Form into balls and gently place in pot of slow boiling water. Cook until all the balls rise to the top of the pot. Remove balls with a slotted spoon.
- Reheat and serve in hot soup (see page 66).

* Ener-G Egg Replacer is a powder that comes in a box. It is available at any natural food store and some supermarkets.

KALE SOUP

A fast, delicious way to prepare kale.

2 tablespoons olive oil
1 or 2 Russet potatoes, roughly diced
2 tablespoons garlic, minced
1 32-ounce Imagine Organic No-chicken broth
1 tablespoon soy sauce
Salt
About 3 cups roughly chopped kale leaves (Strip the leaves from the
    stalk, rinse, and then chop.)

- In a soup pot, add the garlic and the Russet potato to the No-chicken broth. Bring to a boil, then simmer for ten minutes.
- Add the soy sauce and the kale to the simmering broth, and cook about 5 minutes. Taste, add a little more soy sauce if necessary, and serve.

Serves 4 to 5

Steddas

Steddas are the foods that vegetarians have created or discovered that are used instead of something that has animal products in it. Everywhere that vegetarians are cooking, they have been creative in finding ways to replace an ingredient and continue to eat meals they had always enjoyed. Vegetarians who are eating healthily don't have to give up macaroni and cheese or lasagna or cheese spreads or scrambled eggs—they just use different ingredients. If you love burritos made with scrambled eggs, just learn how to make scrambled tofu and use that instead. If you love crackers and cheese try "Chick Cheez" on crackers or bread. If you have recipes that call for buttermilk, just do the same thing you do for the biscuits in this book—clabber soymilk with vinegar. If you like stuffed shells use creamy tofu ricotta, instead. So simple, so quick. Steddas will soon become your steady companions.

Top Ten Stedda Recipes

1. Tofu ricotta (see page 100)
2. Cheezy Sauce (see page 146)
3. Tofu "cottage cheese" (see page 86)
4. Scrambled tofu (see page 47)
5. Chick Cheez (see page 72)
6. Cashew Cream Sauce (see page 143)
7. "Butter"milk (see page 48).
8. Cream pies made from tofu (see for example Chocolate Crème Pie page 115)
9. Tofu benedict (see page 148, tip number 7)
10. Mushroom Stroganoff (see page 87)

CHICK CHEEZ

2 cups drained cooked or canned chickpeas (one 15- or 16-ounce can)

3 tablespoons nutritional yeast flakes

2 tablespoons sesame tahini or raw cashew butter

2 tablespoons fresh lemon juice or white wine vinegar

1 1/2 tablespoons light or chickpea miso

1 to 2 tablespoons extra-virgin olive oil

1 teaspoon onion powder

3/4 teaspoon salt

1/2 teaspoon paprika

1/4 teaspoon garlic powder

1/4 teaspoon dry mustard

- Combine all ingredients in a food processor fitted with a metal blade.
- Process into a smooth paste, stopping to scrape down sides of work bowl as necessary.
- Chill several hours or overnight before serving to allow flavors to blend.

Keeps 5 to 7 days in the refrigerator.

From *The Ultimate Uncheese Cookbook* by Jo Stepaniak. Used with permission.

Sandwiches

⊗

Ten Secrets for Terrific Sandwiches

1. Sauté an onion in barbecue sauce and use in your sandwich.
2. Steam and mash your favorite veggies. Add to the barbecued onion.
3. Add arugula, sliced radishes, or raddichio to a sandwich.
4. Try some fancy mustards like Dijon or horseradish mustard.
5. Find an artisan bread or use a flavored wrap.
6. Add something sweet like a sliced apple or pear or baked or steamed sweet potato.
7. Spread a little baba ghanoush or hummus.
8. Use Tofutti Cream Cheese.
9. Sprinkle in some nuts or small cooked legumes (yes . . . tasty!).
10. Add avocado—it always adds a wonderful taste and texture.

Some of our favorite combinations:
- Barbecued onions plus steamed broccoli plus pickle plus avocado in a wrap.
- Marinated tofu with olives, tomato, lettuce, avocado, sprouts, and pesto on bread.
- Tofu scramble, onions, red bell peppers, potatoes, avocado with salsa in a wrap.
- Peanut butter or a nut butter and banana.
- Chick Cheez plus chopped olives (warm).

- Baked eggplant with tahini on toast.
- Tofu steaks with lettuce, tomato, onion and avocado.
- Hummus, tomato and avocado in pita bread.
- Grilled or roasted veggies in crusty rolls with pesto.
- "It doesn't taste like tofu" dip with lettuce.
- Tahini, sauerkraut, mustard (and if you want, avocado).
- Steamed greens with barbecued onions and mustard.
- Broiled portobello mushrooms used instead of burgers.

RED PEPPER/CASHEW SPREAD

This is an extremely easy to make and popular spread. You can make a low fat version by substituting chickpeas for the cashews.

1 cup raw cashew pieces
1 large red pepper, roasted (You can buy these in a jar or roast your own.)
1/2 cup water as needed and/or the liquid from the jar of roasted peppers

- Combine nuts and pepper in a food processor and add about two or three tablespoons of liquid as needed to process smoothly.
- Scrape down sides of bowl, and continue to add liquid until creamy consistency is reached.

You will have to process the nuts and pepper and liquid for a long time, perhaps as much as 3 full minutes for the texture to become smooth.

SUN-DRIED TOMATO PASTE

1 large handful sun-dried tomatoes, soaked in hot water for a few minutes
   (save the water)
1/2 to 1 clove garlic, depending on how much you like garlic
1 teaspoon olive oil (optional)
Salt to taste
Pepper to taste
1/4 teaspoon dried basil or a few leaves fresh basil

- Combine all ingredients in a blender and blend for a few seconds until a paste is formed.
- Add soaking water by the teaspoon if mixture is too thick.
- Use on top of polenta. Or mix with some vegan cream cheese for a dip.

Makes enough for two servings over pasta or two small pizzas

Do Vegetarians Have to Eat Tofu?

Foods ending in vowels, like tofu and miso, always sound so strange. Most meat foods don't end with vowels. But don't let that keep you from discovering miso and tofu, and tofu's cousin, tempeh. These, as well as other soybean products, are a great way to get bean products into your diet without having to eat the whole bean. But you don't have to like tofu to be a vegetarian. A lot of people swear by it and love it, but you don't have to eat it; you can eat soybeans from a can, or you can eat edamame (the fresh soybean), which is now available in the frozen section of grocery stores.

There is nothing magical about tofu; it's simply that it is made of soybeans and is able to take on a variety of tastes depending on what 't is asked to do in a recipe.

You've wanted to try it. You've bought it. And then tossed it when it reached the expiration date. That's your recipe for tofu: purchase, refrigerate, then toss. There's something discomforting about trying something new. We provide a way to dive into two of these "strange" foods all at once. If the recipe for "It Doesn't Taste like Tofu" dip weren't so great, maybe we wouldn't ask this of you. But if you are going to try one strange food, then this recipe is worth it. Carol makes it every year during the December holiday season (she calls it "holiday pâté") and everyone loves it. It's easy, quick, and keeps for several days. You can use it with fresh veggies as a dip, with crackers, in pita bread as a sandwich, or you can also simply dip your spoon into its creamy substance and enjoy it on its own. By steaming the tofu, you remove some of the beany taste of tofu, and thus eliminate one of the main things that makes people uncomfortable with the idea of eating tofu.

Think of tofu as being like a painter's canvas. Before the painter begins, an endless variety of options exist for the creation that will occur on the canvas. The same can be said of tofu; what people mistake as "bland" is actually the tofu's potential for becoming something new. The cook's creativity will liberate the tofu into its potential, just as the artist liberates the canvas into a work of art.

Tofu can be grilled, broiled, steamed, sautéed, or puréed as a dip.

Tofu can be marinated and then thrown into a salad or marinated and then baked, grilled, broiled or sautéed.

Tofu can be a part of a sandwich; the base for a meal (see "The Life-Saving, Time-Saving, No-Recipe Dinner Formula").

Tofu can be thrown into the ingredients for making hummus to create a creamy alternative; it can be added to a smoothie. It can substitute for eggs and cream cheese for a delicious chocolate crème pie.

Or not. Some vegetarians don't eat tofu; so if you want to eat like a vegetarian, it's not necessary to include tofu in your diet. But, then, there are many wonderful reasons to do so; as many reasons as there are recipes.

The key to trying tofu the first time is don't refrigerate it! Use it the day you buy it. Otherwise, as each day of refrigeration passes, that dependable old recipe (buy, refrigerate, toss) will become more and more attractive.

MARINATED TOFU AND TOFU STEAKS

A simple way to prepare tofu is to slice it into 6 slices (or cut it in half and slice each half in thirds. You can also further cut these slices into half and make triangles). Marinate the slices and then bake them. Voila! Tofu steaks. Use extra-firm (not silken) tofu for tofu steaks.

TEN MARINADES FOR TOFU

1. Soy sauce, orange juice, garlic, and ginger
2. Lemon juice, balsamic vinegar, soy sauce, fresh rosemary
3. Soy sauce and wine vinegar
4. Soy sauce and maple syrup
5. Fat-free vinaigrette with a little added vinegar
6. Tandoori marinade plus plain soy yogurt (both can be bought at grocery stores)
7. Soy sauce, cider vinegar, Pickapeppa sauce, and hot sauce
8. Hoisin sauce, mirin (rice vinegar), soy sauce, brown sugar, ketchup, and garlic
9. Coconut milk, soy sauce, green curry paste, chopped ginger, cloves, and cilantro
10. Red wine, tomato paste, molasses, soy sauce, cayenne pepper, and liquid smoke

- Place the tofu in the marinade and leave for an hour or more. You can leave it overnight, and some leave it for several days!
- Place parchment paper on a pan, put tofu on top and bake at 350°F for 30 to 40 minutes, turning once.

GLAZES FOR TOFU

Some people don't believe tofu has to be marinated; they simply glaze it and bake or broil it. Here are some wonderful glazes:

- Barbecue sauce
- 1/4 cup mellow white or chickpea miso plus 2 tablespoons frozen orange juice concentrate
- Satay sauce (you can buy at supermarkets and natural food stores)
- Hot mustard, molasses, cayenne, minced garlic, and onion
- Thai curry paste and soy sauce

Spread the glaze on the tofu (top with sesame seeds or ground walnuts or nutritional yeast). If you broil the tofu, watch it closely; it requires just a few minutes on each side.

THE "IT DOESN'T TASTE LIKE TOFU" DIP

1 pound of tofu
1 cup grated carrots
1/2 cup scallions
4 tablespoons tahini
2 tablespoons sweet white miso
4 teaspoons tamari

- Put the water on to boil.
- Open the tofu container, empty the water, remove the tofu, and cut it into two.
- When the water is boiling, place the two halves of the tofu onto a steamer. Steam the tofu for 10 minutes.
- While the tofu steams, prepare the carrots and scallions. Run two or so carrots through the food processor's grater (to make the equivalent of 1 cup of carrots). Remove the carrots from the food processor.
- Chop scallions by hand to make 1/2 cup scallions.
- Let the tofu cool a little, then crumble it and place in the food processor fitted with a metal blade.
- Add the tahini, sweet white miso, and tamari. Process into a thick paste.
- Add the carrot and scallions and pulse until they are evenly distributed.
- Transfer to a storage container and chill several hours before serving.

Makes about 2 cups

Adapted from a recipe by Jo Stepaniak

TOFU "COTTAGE CHEESE"

1 pound tofu
1 tablespoon apple cider vinegar
2 tablespoons lemon juice
1 1/2 tablespoons minced onion
1 tablespoon minced chives
2 teaspoons minced dill
2 tablespoons nutritional yeast
1/2 teaspoon salt

- Blend half of the tofu and the other ingredients in a blender or food processor until creamy. Transfer to a bowl.
- Mash the remaining tofu with a fork and then mix into the blended ingredients. Combine well. Adjust seasonings and refrigerate.

Makes about 2 cups

Mushroom Stroganoff

Here's a way to add tofu to a meal without anyone realizing they are getting soy protein!

1 onion, chopped
1 pound mushrooms, sliced
3 Portobello mushroom caps, sliced
2 tablespoons olive oil
4 tablespoons vegetable broth powder or UnChicken stock powder
1/4 teaspoon freshly ground nutmeg
1 1/2 teaspoon soy sauce
1/2 teaspoon mustard powder
1 15-ounce can garbanzo beans
2 teaspoons apple cider vinegar
10 ounces noodles or 1 cup brown rice
1 12-ounce box soft silken tofu

- Warm the oil and, over medium heat, sauté the onions and mushrooms until they are soft (about 10 minutes.)
- Add the broth powder, seasonings, garbanzo beans, and vinegar. Cover and simmer over low heat for about 10 minutes.
- Meanwhile, in a separate large pot, cook the noodles until al dente or boil the rice.
- Empty the tofu into a blender, add some of the liquid from the mushroom mixture. Blend until the tofu is creamy. (But don't taste! The seasonings are with the mushrooms, and this will taste, as it is, rather bland.)

- Add the creamed tofu to the mushroom mixture, and over very low heat, warm the mixture until heated through.
- Serve over cooked noodles or rice.

Serves 4

Dinner Possibilities

❂

POLENTA

Polenta can be served warm or cold, soft or hardened. Patti usually lets it harden in a serving dish. She likes to garnish it with anything colorful. Her favorite toppings are a dollop of salsa or guacamole, or pesto or sun-dried tomato paste. For garnish, a sprig of fresh parsley works, or an olive or a slice of tomato. If she's serving polenta to guests, and bringing the whole pan to the table, she'll cut it into diamonds and alternate pesto and sun-dried tomato paste, for an Italian meal, or guacamole and salsa, for a Mexican meal. Also, she sometimes adds chopped roasted red pepper (from a jar) to the polenta as it cooks, or chopped fresh parsley or both. This makes an especially colorful polenta, as specks of green and red dot the yellow polenta.

Make the polenta first, and as it cools and hardens, make the pesto.

4 cups water
1 cup polenta (coarse corn meal)
1/4 teaspoon salt (You could stop here if you don't have any of the following ingredients.)
1 clove garlic, crushed or chopped
1/4 cup nutritional yeast flakes
1 to 2 teaspoons sage
1 to 2 teaspoons marjoram

1/4 teaspoon salt

1/4 teaspoon black pepper

1/4 cup roasted red pepper from a jar (optional)

Fresh, chopped parsley (optional)

- Put all ingredients except polenta into a pot. When it boils, add polenta slowly, while whisking (stirring in circles with a whisk).
- Continue to whisk (or stir with a large fork) frequently until mixture thickens (about 5 to 8 minutes) and then let it "percolate" for another 10 minutes or so, stirring occasionally. This can splash and hurt you, so use a lid as a shield when approaching the pot.
- Turn off heat and pour mixture, which should be thick, into a quiche pan or a glass, baking dish.
- Let cool (at least 20 minutes).
- Slice as a pie (if in quiche pan) or into diamonds (if in a baking dish). To slice in diamond shapes, make diagonal cuts across the length of the polenta in the pan and then vertical cuts across those.
- Serve warm or cold, garnished with anything colorful.

Serves 6

STUFFED EGGPLANT

1 large eggplant or 3 small eggplants

1 tablespoon olive oil

2 onions, chopped

2 garlic cloves, minced

2 bell peppers, diced

1 1/2 cups chopped tomatoes

3 tablespoons chopped parsley

1/4 teaspoon basil

1 teaspoon salt

2 tablespoons olive oil, Spectrum spread, or margarine

1/2 cup walnuts, chopped

1/2 cup wheat germ

- Preheat the oven to 350°F.
- Slice the eggplant(s) in half lengthwise and scoop out the insides, leaving a 1/4-inch thick shell.
- Place the shells, cut sides down, in an oil-sprayed baking dish and bake until they just begin to soften about 20 minutes.
- Coarsely chop the eggplant flesh.
- Heat the oil in a large non-stick skillet and add the chopped eggplant, onions, garlic, and bell peppers. Cook over medium heat, stirring often, until the eggplant begins to soften, about 10 minutes (add a small amount of water if necessary to prevent sticking).
- Add the tomatoes, parsley, basil, and salt. Cook over medium heat until the eggplant is tender when pierced with a fork, about 10 minutes.

- Divide the mixture among the eggplant shells.
- Mix the Spectrum spread or melted margarine (or olive oil) with the walnuts and wheat germ. Spread evenly over the eggplant shells.
- Arrange the shells in one or two baking dishes. Bake until the shells are tender when pierced with a fork, about 45 minutes. Serve with brown rice or basmati and wild rice pilaf.

Serves 6

From *The Peaceful Palate* by Jennifer Raymond. Used with permission.

RED LENTILS AND CHICKPEAS

1 teaspoon mustard seeds
1 teaspoon cumin seeds
1 teaspoon olive oil
1 onion, diced
2 cups water
1/2 cup red lentils
Optional: 1 cup chickpeas

- In a dry pot, toast mustard seeds and cumin seeds until they pop.
- When they start smelling fragrant or begin popping add the olive oil and onion.
- Sauté the onion for a minute with the now warm and fragrant spices.
- Add 2 cups of water and 1/2 cup lentils
- Bring the water to boil.
- Cook until it turns into a yellow mush.
- Add chickpeas, if you wish.

Serves 2

TERRY'S OMEGA-3 PATTIES

Terry Jensen is an activist in Dallas, who coordinates the Dallas-Fort Worth Vegetarian Education Network. She is an innovative cook, and committed to helping people eat healthfully.

3 cups Ranch Style Black Beans, drained (see note, below)
1/4 cup walnut pieces
1/4 cup ground flax seed
1/4 cup grated zucchini or carrots
2 teaspoon Italian seasoning, ground
1/8 teaspoon garlic powder
Reserved liquid from beans, 1 to 3 tablespoons, as needed.

- Drain black beans, reserving liquid, and mash 3 cups.
- Add remaining ingredients except reserved liquid. Mix well.
- Add reserved liquid, one tablespoon at a time, until mixture holds together but is firm. Form patties the size you prefer.
- Wipe skillet with canola oil.
- Cook patties five minutes per side.
- Serve as a burger with all the fixin's (tomato, lettuce, onion, pickles, etc).

Note: Any soft canned black beans will suffice. Some canned beans, such as Kroger's brand, are not soft enough. But any black beans with a dash of Tabasco or your favorite Mexican hot sauce will work

Makes about 6 patties

BROCCOLI AND AVOCADO ON BROWN RICE

This easy meal is like avocado sushi without the seaweed. It is also great with quinoa instead of rice, and with any other vegetables.

1 cup broccoli florets
1 cup brown rice
2 cups water
1 tablespoon ume vinegar* or more to taste
2 tablespoon sesame seeds
1/2 avocado, cut into small chunks

- In a saucepan, bring water to boil. Add rice and simmer, covered for 20 minutes.
- Add broccoli florets and recover, cooking until water is absorbed, about 10 minutes more.
- Toast sesame seeds on a tray in a toaster oven or in a dry frying pan, only until fragrant. Do not burn.
- Place cooked rice and broccoli in a bowl.
- Add avocado.
- Sprinkle with ume vinegar and toasted sesame seeds.

Serves 3 to 4

* Ume vinegar is a tasty Japanese vinegar that you can find in many natural food stores.

Indian Lentils with Broccoli and Cauliflower

2 1/2 cups water
1 cup red lentils
1/2 teaspoon cumin
1/2 teaspoon ginger
1/2 teaspoon coriander
1 cup broccoli florets
1 cup cauliflower florets

- Bring water to a boil in a saucepan.
- Add lentils and herbs and cook about 20 minutes until red lentils turn yellow and mushy.
- Add vegetables and cook for an additional 5 minutes.

Serve over cooked brown basmati rice or any other whole grain rice.

Serves 3 to 4

Braised Kale and Collards

Ume vinegar is salty and tangy, but any vinegar will work when braising greens. If you do not use ume vinegar, you may want to add salt just before serving.

1/2 cup water
4 to 6 large collard leaves
5 to 10 kale leaves
2 cloves garlic (or more to taste), chopped
2 tablespoons ume vinegar* or any other vinegar
salt to taste (if not using ume vinegar)

- Wash kale and collard greens, and remove large stems. Chop leaves.
- Bring water to a boil in a saucepan and add leaves, cooking for about 2 minutes.
- Add garlic, and stir leaves and garlic.
- Add vinegar and stir again.
- The greens are ready when they begin to stick to the bottom of the pot, about 5 to 6 minutes total cooking time.

Serves 2

* Ume vinegar is a tasty Japanese vinegar that you can find in many natural food stores.

LASAGNA

Many lasagna recipes take a long time to prepare. This one saves time by using tomato sauce from a jar, and by not precooking the noodles. The extra water helps the noodles cook while they are baking. If you want to "doctor" the jar of sauce, feel free to add anything you like: mushrooms, garlic, more oregano, basil, onion, sun-dried tomatoes. If you make the tofu ricotta in advance, you'll save an extra five minutes.

One of the benefits of vegetarian cooking is that most recipes are very forgiving. While it's difficult to make lasagna without tomato sauce, noodles, and some sort of "cheese" layer, virtually every other ingredient is optional. So if you don't have zucchini, you can still make this recipe. You can substitute diced peppers or mushrooms or grated carrots, or just skip that ingredient altogether. Carol uses sliced, sautéed Portobello mushrooms. The same goes for the garlic, oregano, spinach, and paprika. And if you don't have tofu, but you happen to have a commercial vegan cheese in the fridge, use what you have. Don't skip a recipe just because you're missing one or two ingredients. While it's always safe to follow the recipe, by improvising and experimenting you make the recipe your own; substitute what you have on hand.

1 package lasagna noodles (whole wheat when available)
1 24- or 25-ounce jar tomato sauce
1 1/2 cups water
2 or more cloves garlic, minced (optional)
1 batch tofu ricotta (see page 100)
1 zucchini, grated
1 package frozen, chopped spinach, thawed

1 tablespoon oregano

2 teaspoons paprika

- Make the tofu ricotta (see page 100)
- Preheat oven to 350°F.
- Mix the water and the tomato sauce to make a thinner sauce.
- Ladle a layer of the thin tomato sauce on the bottom of a 9 x 13-inch baking dish.
- Cover with a layer of noodles. (Usually, you will have to break some noodles so they fit all the way to the edges of the pan.)
- Sprinkle the tofu ricotta evenly over the noodles. (Don't try to be too even-handed; it will be unevenly covered, and that's okay.)
- Sprinkle half the grated zucchini and half the frozen spinach over the ricotta layer.
- Sprinkle half the oregano and half the garlic over this layer.
- Add a generous layer of the tomato sauce, and another layer of noodles.
- Repeat the layers of tofu ricotta, zucchini and spinach, oregano and garlic, and tomato sauce, ending with noodles on top covered with tomato sauce and a little tofu ricotta.
- Sprinkle the paprika over the whole dish.
- Cover with parchment paper and foil, and bake covered for 35 minutes. Uncover and bake an additional 10 to 15 minutes.

Makes one pan to serve about 8 to 10

RICH AND CREAMY TOFU RICOTTA

1 pound tofu
3 tablespoons extra-virgin olive oil
2 tablespoons lemon juice
1/2 teaspoon salt
2 garlic cloves peeled
1 teaspoon mellow barley miso
1 tablespoon fresh rosemary, finely chopped

- In a food processor fitted with a metal blade, combine the tofu, oil, lemon juice, salt, garlic and miso.
- Process, stopping a few times to scrape down the sides, until the tofu is smooth with a slightly granular texture.
- Add the chopped rosemary and pulse to combine.
- Remove from the processor. Use in lasagna, manicotti, and ravioli.

Enough for one large lasagna pan

ROASTED VEGETABLES WITH GARLIC AND FENNEL SEEDS

1/4 cup olive oil

1 tablespoon crushed garlic

1 tablespoon fennel seeds

1/2 teaspoon salt and a pinch of ground black pepper

1 1/2 pounds of butternut squash, peeled and cut into 1-inch chunks.

1 1/2 pounds of carrots, cut into 1-inch chunks.

1 pound small red onions, quartered

- Preheat oven to 425°F.
- Mix 1 tablespoon of the olive oil with the garlic and fennel seeds and set aside.
- Toss each vegetable with some of the remaining olive oil and some salt and pepper. Place vegetables on a large baking sheet, with the harder vegetables around the outside, surrounding the softer vegetables. Bake the vegetables for 15 minutes.
- Stir, loosening them if they have begun to stick to the pan. Roast 15 minutes longer or until they are tender when a fork pierces them.
- Toss the vegetables with the olive oil/garlic/fennel seed mixture. Roast for 8 minutes. When two minutes are left, toss the vegetable with the chopped parsley and balsamic vinegar. Remove from the oven.

You will enjoy variations of this recipe throughout cold winter months.

Serves 6

From *Professional Vegetarian Cooking* by Ken Bergeron. Used with permission.

ROASTED POTATOES

About 10 small potatoes (red, yellow, fingerling, etc.)
1 teaspoon oregano
1 teaspoon basil
1 teaspoon sage
1 teaspoon thyme
Olive oil spray (or about ¼ teaspoon olive oil)
Optional: salt to taste

- Preheat oven to 400°F.
- Wash potatoes and quarter them. Spray with olive oil (or toss with olive oil) and add all herbs. Toss to mix.
- Spread on a cookie sheet and bake for 20 minutes.
- Turn them over and bake an additional 20 minutes or until potatoes are golden brown.

Serves 4

ORZO PILAF

2 cups water

1 cup orzo

2 tablespoons UnChicken vegetable broth powder

4 tablespoons nutritional yeast

Teaspoon garlic-infused olive oil

- Bring water to boil.
- As water is coming to boil, shake orzo in a jar with the broth powder.
- Add the orzo to the water, and return to a boil.
- Lower the heat, add the nutritional yeast, and cook covered until all water is absorbed, about 15 minutes.
- Toss with olive oil.
- Optional: Stir in some sautéed mushrooms after you remove the orzo from the heat.

Serves 4

STUFFED ACORN SQUASH

A great Thanksgiving dish.

4 small acorn squashes (no more than one pound each)
Oil

For the Stuffing
2 tablespoons olive oil
1 cup onions, finely chopped
2 cups mushrooms, sliced
1 cup celery, finely chopped
4 cloves garlic, minced
2 teaspoons poultry seasoning (or 1/4 teaspoon each of marjoram, rosemary, thyme, sage, and basil)
3 tablespoons tamari soy sauce
1/2 teaspoon sea salt
3 cups whole wheat bread, cubed (Be sure to select a bread that wasn't baked with eggs, milk, cheese, or whey.)
1/2 cup fresh parsley, chopped
1/2 cup chopped dried apricots (for a real treat use glacé [sweetened] apricots)
Optional: add roasted chestnuts

- Preheat the oven to 350°F.
- Cut the squashes in half across the width of the squash. Scoop the seeds out. Lightly coat the edges of the squash with oil, place on a baking sheet cut side down, and bake for about 40 minutes.

- Remove from the oven.
- Meanwhile, prepare the stuffing. Heat the oil in a large nonstick frying pan over medium heat. Add onions, mushrooms, celery, garlic. Stir. Sprinkle poultry seasoning over vegetables. Dissolve the salt in the tamari/soy sauce and add to the pan. Stir, then cover, and continue to cook until the vegetables are done, about five minutes. Remove from heat.
- Add the cubed bread, parsley, and apricots. Mix well. Then cover and set aside for several minutes. The bread should absorb the moisture from the vegetables. The stuffing should be well seasoned and moist, but not wet.
- The recipe can be prepared to this point ahead of time.
- Just before serving, stuff each squash with about 1/2 cup of stuffing. Bake in a 375°F oven for about 15 to 20 minutes, until thoroughly heated.

Makes 4 cups of stuffing
Serves 8 people as a main dish, and 16 as a side dish

SCALLOPED POTATOES

4 cups potatoes, peeled and thinly sliced
2 medium onions, chopped
1/3 cup flour
1/3 cup margarine
2 quarts soymilk or combination of soymilk and UnChicken stock

- Preheat oven to 350°F.
- Oil a 9 x 13-inch pan.
- Put a layer of sliced potatoes on the bottom, add onions, sprinkle some flour over the vegetables, and a little salt and pepper. Dot with a little of the margarine.
- Repeat, making several layers. Omit flour when you reach the top layer.
- Pour soymilk or soymilk/UnChicken stock combination slowly over the vegetables until the top layer is almost covered.
- Bake for 1 1/2 to 2 hours, until the potatoes are soft when tested with a fork and the soymilk is thickened.

Serves 6

POTATO PANCAKES (LATKES)

In Patti's house, Hanukkah is the only time she fries food, and this is virtually the only thing she fries. This recipe serves two hungry people if it's the whole meal, or six people who show more restraint than she can muster. The aroma lingers in the house for days, reminding her of her grandmother who made these for her year-round, every time she would visit. She made the pancakes with eggs and sugar, neither of which proves necessary. Patti always eat these with applesauce, but some families prefer sour cream, a vegan version of which you can make or buy.

The same recipe can be made with sweet potatoes instead of Russet potatoes. Adding a teaspoon of cinnamon with the sweet potatoes is a nice touch.

4 Russet potatoes, peeled
2 large yellow onions
1 cup matzoh meal
2 teaspoons pepper
2 teaspoons salt
lots of olive oil and canola oil
applesauce or vegan sour cream

- Grate the potatoes and onions and combine in a large bowl. Add matzoh meal, pepper, and salt. Mix well with your hands.
- In a large frying pan heat about 1/4 cup olive and canola oil combined. (The canola keeps the oil from smoking; Patti used to use only olive oil and the smoke alarm went off every time.)
- Make patties of the potato mixture, squeezing out excess liquid as

you form them. Place each pancake gently into the hot oil. When the edges turn brown, turn gently with a spatula and cook the second side for about 2 minutes, until light brown.

- Drain on the inside of brown paper grocery bags, cut open.
- Serve with applesauce or vegan sour cream.

Makes 25 small pancakes

MAC DADDY

This recipe from Isa Chandra Moskowitz and Terry Hope Romero can serve a houseful; it is tasty and filling! The original recipe's idea to use mashed tofu in addition to their Cheezy sauce with the macaroni did give it more of the old fashioned "mac 'n' cheese" taste and texture. Sprinkling some breadcrumbs on top wouldn't hurt! Or even breadcrumbs with a little additional nutritional yeast and some chopped parsley. You can freeze this dish, or a part of it, and it still tastes great.

Double recipe Cheezy sauce (see page 146)
3/4 pound elbow macaroni
1 pound extra-firm tofu
1 teaspoon salt
1 tablespoon olive oil
2 tablespoons fresh lemon juice

- Bring a large pot of salted water to a boil.
- Add the macaroni and cook according to the package directions, about 10 minutes.
- Meanwhile, prepare your Cheezy sauce.
- Preheat the oven to 325°F. When the pasta is ready, drain and set aside. When sauce is ready, begin assembling.

To assemble
- Crumble the tofu into an 11 x 13-inch glass or ceramic baking dish.
- Mash the tofu with your hands until it resembles ricotta cheese. Add the salt, olive oil, and lemon juice, then stir.

- Add 1/2 cup Cheezy sauce to the tofu and stir. Use a dry measuring cup with a handle so that you can just dip it in to the sauce and pour—you don't need to be very precise.
- Add the macaroni to the tofu, along with 3 more cups of sauce, and stir well.
- Smooth the top of the pasta mixture and press it down with a spatula to level it. Then pour the remaining sauce over the pasta and smooth again.
- Bake for 30 minutes; the top of the macaroni should be slightly browned.
- It's a good idea to wait for about 20 minutes before serving, so that it can cool down and firm up a bit, but if you can't wait, more power to you.

Serves 8 to 10

- **Variations**
  - *Mac and Peas*: Add 2 cups of frozen peas when you add the macaroni to the casserole.
  - *Broc Mac Daddy*: Add 3 cups of small broccoli florets when you add the macaroni.
  - *Autumn Mac Daddy*: Add 3 cups of roasted or boiled butternut squash when you add the macaroni. Omit the thyme from the nutritional yeasty sauce and add 1 teaspoon of ground nutmeg.
  - *Spicy Mac Daddy*: Add 3/4 teaspoon of red pepper flakes to the nutritional yeasty sauce when you add the black pepper.
  - *Mac and Greens*: Add 4 cups of finely chopped kale, spinach, or chard when you add the macaroni.

⌒ *Mac and Chicks*: Instead of tofu, use 2 cups of mashed chickpeas.

From *Veganomicon: The Ultimate Vegan Cookbook* by Isa Chandra Moskowitz and Terry Hope Romero. Used with permission.

Sweets

❦

THE BEST SCONE RECIPE IN THE WORLD

Everyone needs a treat!

This scone recipe creates hands-down the most popular food that emerges from Carol's kitchen. It can be used as an after-school snack, a morning breakfast treat, or a dessert. Because it uses so much less sugar and fat than chocolate chip cookies, it is a healthier way to treat anyone to chocolate desserts. And its biggest attraction is that, if you have the ingredients on hand, it can be whipped up in minutes. Mixing baking soda and vinegar causes a volcano-like explosion in elementary school science demonstrations; they perform the same function here, giving the scones a light and airy texture.

Serve the scones warm, or soon thereafter.

1 tablespoon apple cider vinegar
Approximately 1 cup soymilk
3 teaspoons vanilla extract
1/2 cup Spectrum spread or margarine like Earth Balance

Dry ingredients:
1 1/2 cups unbleached all-purpose flour
1 1/2 cups spelt flour or whole wheat pastry flour
3/8 cup Sucanat or turbinado sugar
3 teaspoons baking powder

3/4 teaspoon baking soda
3/4 teaspoon salt

For chocolate chip scones:
1 cup chocolate chips

For our favorite non-chocolate scones:
1/2 cup toasted walnuts, coarsely chopped
1/2 cup dried cherries, crystallized ginger or dried cranberries
1/2 cup carob chips

- Place the rack in the middle of the oven.
- Preheat the oven to 425°F.
- Use a nonstick cookie sheet lightly misted with vegetable oil cooking spray or line a cookie sheet with parchment paper.
- Put the tablespoon of apple cider vinegar into a 1-cup measuring cup and add enough soymilk to bring it level to a cup. Set aside.
- In a large mixing bowl, mix together the dry ingredients.
- Add the Spectrum spread or margarine to the dry ingredients, and cut it in using a pastry blender or two knives or your fingers. The mixture will be crumbly now.
- Add the chocolate or the carob/walnut/cherry mixture to the mixing bowl and mix them in.
- Add the vanilla to the soymilk mixture and pour almost all of this mixture into the dry ingredients.
- Stir quickly with a spatula only until the mixture forms a soft dough. You don't want a gooey mess, so only add more soymilk if the dough still seems crumbly rather than doughy.

- Turn the dough onto the cookie sheet in 4 equal parts. Shape each part into a thick circle about 5 to 7 inches in diameter. Using a sharp knife, score the top of each circle, dividing it into quarters.
- Bake for 12 minutes. A toothpick stuck into the middle of each scone should come out clean, and the bottoms will be lightly browned. Don't let them bake too long. Transfer them to a wire rack, break into pieces where scored, and enjoy.

For 16 large scones

- Variations:
  - Chocolate chips, walnuts, and crystallized ginger
  - Dried apricots, walnuts, and chocolate chips
  - Dried blueberries, almonds, and chocolate chips
  - Scones a-la-mode: Cut the scone in half and dollop some of your favorite non-dairy ice cream on top, followed by some chocolate sauce.

Adapted from *Short-Cut Vegetarian* by Lorna Sass

CHOCOLATE CRÈME PIE

We take this to church socials, feed hungry teens with it, and use it for birthday celebrations. No one can believe it has tofu in it.

2 boxes firm silken tofu
1 1/2 to 2 cups vegan chocolate chips
1 tablespoon vanilla
1 large size graham crust
Fruit (optional)

- Melt the chocolate chips over low heat, stirring constantly.
- Put the silken tofu in a food processor and process.
- Add the melted chocolate chips and process until smooth.
- Add the vanilla and process.
- Pour into the crust and refrigerate for a couple of hours.
- Add strawberries, kiwi, or other fruits to the top if you wish. But no fruits are necessary for this delicious dessert.

Serves 6 to 8

GINGERBREAD

Jennifer Raymond writes: "This gingerbread contains no animal ingredients and no added fat, yet it is moist and delicious. Try serving it with hot applesauce for a real treat." It is a great recipe. We sometimes add chocolate chips for a treat. Makes one 9 x 9-inch cake.

1/2 cup raisins
1/2 cup pitted dates, chopped
1 3/4 cups water
3/4 cup raw sugar or other sweetener
1/2 teaspoon salt
2 teaspoon cinnamon
1 teaspoon ginger
3/4 teaspoon nutmeg
1/4 teaspoon cloves
2 cups flour (I use whole wheat pastry flour.)
1 teaspoon baking soda
1 teaspoon baking powder

- Combine dried fruits, water, sugar, and seasonings in a large saucepan and bring to a boil. Continue boiling for 2 minutes, then remove from heat and cool completely.
- When fruit mixture is cool, mix in dry ingredients. Spread into a greased 9 x 9-inch pan and bake at 350°F for 30 minutes or until a toothpick inserted into the center comes out clean.

From *The Peaceful Palate* by Jennifer Raymond. Used with permission.

CAROL'S CHOCOLATE CHOCOLATE CHOCOLATE BREAD

Many people who don't cook have a bread machine. If you are one of those, you can make this marvelous chocolate bread, wonderful on its own, or with raspberry jam, or for use in French toast. If there is any left, use it as breadcrumbs for an interesting flavor. Or sauté cubes of it for an interesting crouton. Below you will find the recipe for the bread machine. On the next page you will find a recipe for making it without a bread machine. Since the premise of this book is that you don't have to work hard to eat well as a vegetarian, you might not want to tackle kneading dough and creating a bread by hand. We understand and sympathize! But we also didn't want to deprive you of a wonderful way to have a sweet without having all the fat and sugar that cookies and other sweets often deliver.

The best way to awaken the chocolate flavor in the bread is to toast the bread lightly.

For a variation, make chocolate chocolate dough (leave out the chocolate chips from the bread machine if you use one). Remove the dough and cut it in half. Roll each half out so that it is in a rectangle, just as you would for dough for cinnamon rolls, but instead of spreading the cinnamon mixture on it, sprinkle the chocolate chips all over the dough! Then roll the dough up, slice the roll into 3/4-inch pieces, lay them flat on a baking sheet and bake. Mmmm!

This recipe is for a bread machine.

Dry Ingredients:
3 3/8 cups of flour (Carol often uses 1/4 cup of soy flour, 1 1/2 cups
  whole wheat flour, and the rest bread flour.)

1 teaspoon salt
3 tablespoon cocoa
1 tablespoon gluten
1 1/2 teaspoon yeast

Then add wet ingredients:
1 1/2 tablespoon olive oil
1 1/2 tablespoon molasses
1 7/16 cups chocolate soymilk

- As the mix cycle of the machine begins to combine the flour with the liquids, check to make sure there is enough soymilk. If it isn't forming a large ball, it might need a couple of tablespoons more soymilk.
- When all the flour is mixed in (about five minutes), slowly add: 1/2 to 1 bag of vegan chocolate chips (or 1 to 2 cups) Enjoy!

CAROL'S CHOCOLATE BREAD (WITHOUT A BREAD MACHINE) (ADAPTED BY SHIRLEY WILKES JOHNSON)

1/4 cup warm water with 1 1/2 teaspoons yeast and 1/2 teaspoon sugar added
3 1/4 cups unbleached white flour
1/4 cup soy flour
3 tablespoons unsweetened cocoa powder
1 tablespoon gluten flour
1 cup vegan chocolate chips
1 1/4 cups chocolate soy milk—warm just a little if refrigerated

1 1/2 tablespoons light olive oil

1 1/2 tablespoons molasses

- Allow yeast mixture to sit for about 10 minutes until foamy.
- Meanwhile mix the unbleached white four, soy flour, cocoa, gluten flour, and chocolate chips together in a bowl.
- In a smaller bowl, mix the soymilk, olive oil and molasses.
- Whisk the yeast mixture into the soymilk mixture and stir into the flour mixture, mixing well.
- Knead the dough until you have a nice dough that feels elastic yet soft. If it is sticky or wet, dust with a little flour.
- Place into an oiled bowl and cover with plastic wrap or clean damp kitchen towel. Allow to rise for about an hour. Punch the dough down and form into a loaf and place into a sprayed (with nonstick) loaf pan. Cover with plastic and allow to rise 30 to 45 minutes.
- Bake in a preheated 350°F oven for 40–45 minutes.

Note: If you don't have chocolate soymilk use plain or vanilla flavored and you can add 1/2 tablespoon more of cocoa powder and two tablespoons of sugar to the flour.

Cooking on the Weekend

❖

The secret of eating well without effort is eating leftovers. All you need to do is to cook one day a week, and you will get to eat two, three, or four different meals from that one day of effort.

You might take two hours out of a Sunday afternoon and fix three or four different things. For instance, you might choose to make a major soup or stew, a casserole/loaf, and a grain. Or you could fix polenta, a pot of rice, lentil barley soup, a salad, and hummus. Or you could prepare two salads and two entrées. If you are ambitious you might prepare three salads (perhaps a bean salad, a cabbage salad, and a chopped vegetable salad, or at least prepared crudités). You might prepare two different sauces and one or more pots of whole grain (brown rice, quinoa, kasha, millet). By reheating the soup or the casserole and just steaming veggies every night, you won't have to cook until Thursday.

And here's the real bonus: You only clean up once for all those days of meals. The key is to never wash the pots or the bowls until you are done preparing all the meals. You save time by chopping all the veggies for the different dishes at the same time.

- Don't bother washing out utensils between dishes.
- Prepare four times the amount of salad you want and hold back the wet foods (tomatoes, onions, artichokes).
- As you reheat leftover foods, consider adding a few leaves of kale, collards, or a few broccoli florets.
- To keep salads crisp, do not add any wet ingredients in advance. Just

keep the washed, torn, cut salad greens in a big bowl covered with a dishcloth and plastic. You can add the tomatoes, cucumbers, avocado, and other veggies at the last minute to the portion size you want with your meal.

THE KEY TO SIMPLIFIED COOKING

Choose one day a week to cook:
- 3 salads
- One main course
- One or more pots of whole grain (brown rice, quinoa, kasha, millet, etc.)
- One soup

(For easy recipes see *Fat Free and Easy* or *The Peaceful Palate* by Jennifer Raymond.)

- Pick three entrées, two salads, and two sauces, and you have a delicatessen.
- Every time you heat a leftover, you can create something different by adding new vegetables or spices.

On the next pages, you will find an example of what you can do with one recipe.

JENNIFER'S LENTIL BARLEY SOUP

Thick enough to be called a stew, this hearty soup is made in a single pot. Add more water or stock if you desire a thinner soup.

2 cups lentils (about 1 pound)
3/4 cup pearl barley
8 cups water or vegetable stock
1 large onion, chopped
2 carrots, diced
2 stalks celery, sliced
2 garlic cloves, pressed or crushed
1/2 teaspoon each: oregano, cumin
1/4 teaspoon red pepper flakes
1/4 teaspoon black pepper
1 1/2 teaspoon salt

- Place all ingredients except salt into a large kettle and bring to a simmer.
- Cover and simmer for one hour, stirring occasionally, until lentils and barley are tender.
- Add salt to taste.

Serves 12

From *The Peaceful Palate* by Jennifer Raymond. Used with permission.

Every time you reheat lentil barley soup it will get thicker.

The first time you eat it you can enjoy it as soup. The second time, it will have thickened. You can put it on baked potatoes, or baked yams as a topping. The third time, it will make a great sandwich filler—in pita or hollowed-out French bread. Add some dark greens or onion or tomato if you like.

All you need to enjoy soup a second or third time is the soup itself and something colorful or crunchy. Take whatever is around—tomato, red onion, maybe a few leaves of collard or kale, avocado, sliced celery, fennel, radishes—and add them to the top of the soup or to the "soup sandwich."

"Dragon Bowl": Rice Plus Veggies Plus Sauce

Every vegetarian eventually develops her or his own version of the Dragon Bowl, a term that encompasses dishes with rice as their base, veggies heaped on top, and then a favorite sauce drizzled over the entire dish. Some vegetarians enjoy their dragon bowl in a special bowl dedicated just to this dish. Carol has a wooden bowl from 1975 that continues to play host to her dragon bowls. Patti's favorite version uses ume plum vinegar, avocado, and toasted sesame seeds.

One of the special things about the dragon bowl is that it can be different each time you eat it, depending on what you have at hand. If you are doing your cooking on the weekend, cook up a big pot of brown rice. (We have found that short grain brown rice is crunchy and tasty. Also brown basmati rice has a nutty and aromatic flavor.)

- Ten to fifteen minutes before the rice is done, toss in some leafy greens.
- **Or** prepare your favorite veggies as the rice is cooking.

When the rice is done, you are ready for your dragon bowl. Throughout the week, you can vary your ingredients for the dragon bowl by adding to the veggies or changing the sauce. The Dragon Bowl can be visualized through this formula:

Rice + veggies + tofu steaks (maybe) + sauce = Dragon Bowl

- You can even name your Dragon Bowls:
  - Basic Dragon Bowl might be a very simple dragon bowl featuring some grated or chopped carrots and chopped kale. Let them steam

on top of the rice when the rice is nearly done. Add a tofu steak (see page 83) and top with your favorite garnishes.

- Spring Dragon Bowl would feature spring vegetables like asparagus
- Summer Dragon Bowl would include zucchini, summer squash, peppers, and tomatoes
- Fall Dragon Bowl would highlight a variety of baked squash, like butternut or acorn
- Winter Dragon Bowl might feature root vegetables.
- You can also name them for your favorite sauces:
  - Peanut Dragon Bowl (see page 142)
  - Gravy Dragon Bowl (see page 144)
- Or for the color of your veggies:
  - Green Dragon Bowl (steamed broccoli, bok choy, kale, and Swiss chard)

Carol loves a tahini sauce for her dragon bowl (and often adds sea vegetables as well).

BASIC TAHINI SAUCE

1/2 cup tahini
1/2 cup (or a little more) water
2 tablespoons lemon juice
1 clove garlic
1 tablespoon (or more, to taste) soy sauce
optional: 1/4 cup or more parsley, chopped

- Blend ingredients in a blender or food processor. Or mix by hand.

Even More Basic Tahini Sauce

- Place a couple of tablespoons of tahini on top of your dragon bowl, mix with the veggies and rice and then sprinkle some soy sauce over it.

- Possible Garnishes for Dragon Bowl:
  - chopped cilantro or parsley
  - chopped scallions
  - sesame seeds
  - avocado
  - grated carrots
  - bean sprouts
  - red onions, chopped
  - sundried tomatoes
  - sunflowers sprouts
  - legumes
- When you cook on the weekend, prepare the vegetable garnishes and keep in refrigerator containers, for easy access all week long.

For more variations, see "The Life-Saving, Time-Saving, No-Recipe Dinner Formula" on pages 140–141.

Part Three

Vegetarian Cooking without Recipes

Vegetarian meals can erupt from a summer garden, from an autumn harvest, from a winter's pantry, or a spring's return. Roots, leaves, seeds, stems, grains, beans, and fruit come together to give vegetarians an abundance of tasty, attractive, filling, and nutritious food choices. The best way to enjoy vegetarian meals is by learning how to cook without recipes.

Ten Tips for Cooking without Recipes

1. Use a lot of herbs. Experiment with different combinations and see what you like. For example, marjoram and sage work well together. Toss some fresh rosemary with roasted vegetables. Throw in some parsley, cilantro, basil, oregano, and thyme directly into your salad.
2. If a recipe calls for broth and you don't have broth, use a quarter cup of red lentils in the water. They turn yellow when they cook and can make any soup look and feel like it's broth based.
3. When you taste a dish, if you think something needs more flavor, double what you think is the normal quantity of herbs or add a tiny bit of vinegar or lemon juice.
4. Get a rice cooker: add veggies ten minutes before the rice is done.
5. The principle of stir-fry cooking is to add the "softest" ingredients last, i.e., carrots would be stir-fried before adding mushrooms.
6. Plan a meal around pasta, potato, or grain. Add vegetables and a sauce on top, and dinner is simple.
7. Read cookbooks for fun. You will develop an understanding of which herbs go well together, roughly which kinds of sauces work well with which kinds of pastas, potatoes, or grains. Even if all you remember is the essence of a dish, you can probably create something delicious by playing with the key ingredients in your own way.
8. Follow a new recipe once. Then you will be able to change it according to what you have on hand, what you have time to do, and what appeals to you more.

9. Salads are the easiest foods to prepare without a recipe. Start with any premixed greens and top with sliced or shredded parts of all or any of the vegetables or fruits on hand. Carrots, celery, radishes, jicama, sprouts, cabbage, kale, collards, apples, oranges, pears. Also, any beans from a can, once rinsed, make salads heartier and more fun to chew.

10. Whole foods in their natural state can be a meal in themselves, no cooking required! Try fresh fruit and nuts for breakfast, raw carrots or celery dipped in nut butter for lunch, and a salad for dinner. It's not everyday fare, but it's a good way to build confidence: You CAN eat well without following recipes, and you CAN find creative and satisfying ways to eat well even on the run.

Ten Recipeless Meals

1. Veggie burgers (store bought) on whole wheat rolls with a salad
2. Burritos: tortillas rolled around refried beans, chopped onion, and tomatoes
3. Baked potatoes and veggie topping (sliced mushrooms, onions, shredded soy cheese)
4. Spaghetti and tomato sauce, salad, bread
5. "Whatever is in the refrigerator" soup
6. Rice (or any grain) and steamed veggies topped with your favorite salad dressing ("Dragon Bowl")
7. Pasta topped with store-brought baba ghanoush (an eggplant dip) thinned.
8. Wraps—leftovers rolled in a large tortilla or chapatti
9. Fresh vegetables dipped into any nut butter, or nut butter spread on collard leaves and rolled up
10. Hot or cold cereal with rice or soymilk, topped with fruit, nuts, flax seeds.

BASIC SANDWICHES

Sandwiches are easy without recipes.

1. Select bread/roll/pita pocket/tortilla/"hoagie" roll/bagel or bun
2. Choose the centerpiece to your sandwich: Veggie deli slices/marinated baked tofu/tofu salad/hummus/mock tuna, or any spread
3. Then look through the refrigerator for colorful or crunchy additions. Here are some ideas to mix and match, but feel free to use anything you find:

Avocado/Guacamole	Olives
Tomato	Any thick leftover soup
Sprouts	Red, yellow, or green pepper
Lettuce	Leftover salad
Kale, collards, or spinach	Artichoke hearts
Baby bok choy	Jicama
Radishes	Cucumber
Carrots	Zucchini
Polenta	Mashed yams
Roasted red pepper	Nut butter
Steamed veggies	Mashed, steamed vegetables

● Spread with veg*n mayonnaise/mustard/salsa/horseradish/salad dressing/barbecue sauce/hummus.
● Optional: sprinkle sunflower seeds, walnuts, pine nuts, or other nuts before closing the sandwich or wrapping up the tortilla.

THE PERFECT RECIPELESS SALAD(S)

Start with a mix of greens, including salad greens and some young kale or collards. Add color and crunch in the form of any of the following:

Carrots (shredded or sliced)	Cucumbers
Celery	Tomatoes
Radicchio	Avocado
Red cabbage	Sprouts
Radishes (red or daikon)	Slices of pear or apple
Cooked beets	Walnuts
Sliced fennel	Soybeans
Parsley	Chickpeas
Baby bok choy, chopped	Any colorful bean
Zucchini	Orange or tangerine slices
Yellow squash	Apple slices
Artichoke hearts	Any cooked whole grain

You can add fresh fruit to a green salad right before you eat it. Try slices of apples, pears, tangerine, orange, kiwi, or any other fruit that you like.

Corny Addition

To a salad of mixed greens, add fresh corn kernels straight from the cob. They're sweet, crunchy, colorful, and delicious. And unlike croutons, they are fast, inexpensive, and health promoting. Stand the cob upright in a shallow bowl. With a sharp knife cut the kernels off the cob by cutting down the length of the cob, turning it three or four times to get the whole cob.

A handful of walnuts adds nutrients and flavor to any salad. Sprinkle ground flax seeds on salads for a dose of beneficial Omega-3 fats.

Don't Choose:

If you can't decide between a green salad and a fruit salad, have it both ways in one big bowl. A salad of fresh spinach with red or green onion works well with chunks of papaya. Likewise, tangerines work well with most salad greens. Fresh lime juice or seasoned rice vinegar make tasty, light, easy dressings. To cut a papaya, stand a papaya upright with stem facing up. Slice down each wide side to create an oval/circle. Slice the oval/circle into quarters and, with each section, slice the fruit from its skin. Repeat with the skinny sides, but you won't need to quarter the original sections.

SALAD DRESSINGS

The standard salad dressing, 2 parts oil to 1 part vinegar is fine by itself, but becomes much more interesting as the base for other dressings. You can add garlic or mustard. You can use exotic vinegars. You can use lime or lemon in place of or in addition to the vinegar. Or you can eliminate the oil entirely and save your calories for chocolate! Here are some suggestions for fat-free salad dressings:

- Any bottled fat-free dressing
- Seasoned rice vinegar (optional additions: mustard, garlic, capers)
- Bragg's Liquid Aminos
- Ume vinegar
- Fresh lemon or lime juice

- Watered down hummus (optional: add dash vinegar and/or herbs or spices to taste)
- Salsa
- Guacamole
- Half cooked petite peas and half avocado, (dash of cumin or to taste) or add the juice of one fresh orange or tangerine

"Whatever's in the House" Soup

1. The soup always starts with these (except when there is something absent from the pantry):

8 to 12 cups of water or vegetable stock or combination of the two
1 onion, diced (or a bunch of green onions, chopped) or onion flakes
2 carrots, washed and chopped
2 stalks of celery, chopped
1/2 cup red lentils (which turn yellow and dissolve in the soup)

2. Then look around to see what else is available. You could add:

1 large garnet yam, peeled and diced
1 package frozen green beans
4 cloves of garlic, chopped
About 1/2 cup brown rice
Broccoli florettes or cauliflower florettes

3. And finally add seasonings, usually a variety of dried "Italian" herbs:

About 1 teaspoon marjoram
About 1 teaspoon oregano
About 1 teaspoon basil
About 1/2 teaspoon or less black pepper
About 1/4 teaspoon or less red pepper flakes or cayenne pepper (optional; adds bite)

- When the soup is finished cooking, about 45 minutes at a simmer, you can add about 1 teaspoon salt or less.
- Add leafy greens to soups and stews in the last few minutes of cooking. Or make a dark, green soup by boiling an onion and two peeled potatoes until soft and adding the greens.

Serves 8

SUSHI WITHOUT THE WORK

Some vegetarians love to make sushi, some would love to have the time to make sushi, and some would never consider making it. We've found that one can enjoy the tastes of sushi without the work of layering rice and other ingredients on top of sheets of nori and then rolling it up. We have dispensed with the nori; but even without it, you get the wonderful combination of flavors and the kick of the wasabi. We also recommend using brown rice.

Dulse is a sea vegetable that is often sprinkled on top of food instead of salt. Wasabi is the Japanese horseradish that adds a kick to each bite of sushi. Ume plum vinegar is a Japanese vinegar. Many natural food stores carry these products.

Here is Patti's favorite version of sushi without the work. Toss in a bowl:
- Brown rice + steamed broccoli + avocado + sesame seeds + Ume plum vinegar or soy sauce

Once you get started making sushi without the work, why not innovate further?
- Brown rice + sautéed shitake mushrooms + green onions + sesame seeds + Ume plum vinegar
- Brown rice + roasted eggplant and zucchini + sesame seeds + Ume plum vinegar
- Brown rice + carrots + daikon radish (or a regular radish if that is what you have in the kitchen) + cucumber + sesame seeds + Ume plum vinegar. Slice the veggies very thinly.

The Life-Saving, Time-Saving, No-Recipe Dinner Formula

Dinner is another easy No-Recipe opportunity, but a formula does help.

Think in terms of "pasta, potato, or grain" the way you used to think in terms of "chicken, meat, or fish." Here are some ideas:

One dish rice meal: Brown Basmati rice topped with shredded cabbage, chopped carrots, and steamed kale. Add some soy sauce or Bragg's Liquid Aminos and seasoned rice vinegar just before serving.

One dish warm potato salad meal: Steamed small potatoes (halved or quartered) tossed with frozen corn, steamed, chopped collards (add during last 3 minutes of potatoes steaming), chopped celery, and chopped red pepper. Pour some capers over it and toss with mustard.

One dish pasta meal: One package of any whole grain pasta topped with tomato sauce. Garnish with chopped kale. (You may want to add carrots and/or peas—or a bag of frozen mixed vegetables—to the sauce while warming it.)

It usually takes more time to cook your grains than to steam the veggies. Add the veggies to the top of whatever grain is cooking when there are 8 minutes left to the cooking. When you reheat the grain, add more water, about 1/4 cup of water, and add the veggies and microwave.

You can mix and match from the columns on the next pages to create a delicious, health-promoting dinner. If you serve a green salad along with this dish, it's about as easy and filling as any meal can be.

BASE FOR DISH	VEGGIES (COOKED OR RAW)	TOPPINGS
Any small whole-grain pasta (shells, elbows, corkscrew, etc.)	Cruciferous veggies (broccoli, cauliflower, bok choy, Brussels sprouts, red or green or Napa cabbage)	Seeds or nuts (sesame seeds, sunflower seeds, almonds, walnuts or cashews)
Steamed yams	Carrots	Avocado slices
Steamed yellow or small red potatoes	Peas (snow peas, sugar snap peas, plain old peas)	Soy sauce or Bragg's Liquid Aminos
Brown long grain, short grain, or basmati rice	Dark leafy greens: kale, collards, beet greens, chard	Vinegar (seasoned rice, ume plum, balsamic, red or white wine, apple cider)
Quinoa	Beets (golden or red)	Mirin (sweet Japanese cooking wine)
Millet	Winter or summer squash (winter squash should be cooked)	Peanut sauce (see page 142)
Kasha (toasted buckwheat)	Corn	Tomato sauce (from a jar or homemade)

BASE FOR DISH	VEGGIES (COOKED OR RAW)	TOPPINGS
Polenta (corn meal)	Green beans	"Cream Sauce" (see page 143)
Tortillas	Eggplant	Pesto Sauce (see page 78)
Tofu steaks (see page 83, tip 9 on page 29, or tip 7 on page 31)	Mushrooms	Chick Cheez thinned with water or soymilk (see page 72)
Baked potatoes or baked sweet potatoes	Roasted veggies (see page 101)	Marinade or gravy (see page 144)
		Mustard (hot Chinese, Dijon, mixed with horseradish)
		Wasabi
		Any leftover dressings you like

Remember: Mix and match ingredients from each of the columns for wonderful dinners.

Simple Peanut Sauce

1/3 cup peanut butter
2/3 cup hot water
1 tablespoon soy sauce
1 tablespoon vinegar (cider or seasoned rice)
2 garlic cloves, minced
1/4 teaspoon ginger
1/8 teaspoon cayenne

- Whisk all the ingredients together in a small saucepan, then heat gently until the sauce is smooth and slightly thickened.
- Add more water if the sauce becomes too thick.

Makes 1 cup of sauce. Toss with pasta, use as a dip, or top steamed veggies with this delicious sauce.

From *The Peaceful Palate* by Jennifer Raymond. Used with permission.

CASHEW CREAM SAUCE

1/2 cup cashew butter
2 tablespoons fresh lemon juice
Pinch of salt
1/2 cup water, more or less as needed

- Combine all ingredients in a blender or food processor, using just enough water to make a thick, but smooth sauce.
- Alternatively, combine all the ingredients, except the water, together in a small bowl.
- Gradually stir in enough water to make a thick but pour-able sauce.

Makes 1 cup of sauce

From *The Saucy Vegetarian* by Jo Stepaniak. Used with permission.

HOLIDAY FAT-FREE GRAVY

This fat-free gravy is delicious on potatoes, squash, bread, or rice dressing and any other winter food.

2 quarts vegetable stock
1/3 cup white or light miso
1/3 cup dry white wine or mirin
1/3 cup low sodium soy sauce
1 tablespoon apple cider vinegar
2 to 3 teaspoons poultry seasoning or other mixed herbs (see note)
1/2 to 1 teaspoon dried rosemary
1/2 to 1 teaspoon dried sage
1/2 to 1 teaspoon thyme
1/2 teaspoon black or white pepper
Salt to taste
2 to 3 tablespoons cornstarch or arrowroot as thickener

- Combine all ingredients except cornstarch or arrowroot in a 4-quart pot. Bring to a boil over medium heat, then lower heat and simmer for 10 minutes.
- At serving time, dissolve thickener in 1/2 cup of cold water. Bring the gravy to a low boil.
- Slowly pour in the thickener and stir while the gravy turns from milky to smooth. Add enough thickener to reach the consistency you desire.

Makes 8 cups

Note: Poultry seasoning does not contain animal products. If you don't have poultry seasoning, use 2 to 3 teaspoons of a mixture of dried rosemary, sage, thyme, marjoram, and basil.

Thanks to Ann Wheat for this favorite holiday recipe.

CHEEZY SAUCE

The following are the ingredients that Isa Chandra Moskowitz and Terry Hope Romero recommend for their cheezy sauce. Our taste testers (a teenage boy and a young adult) both felt a little margarine was needed, that the turmeric was absolutely essential, and we also added some Dijon mustard. It's a versatile sauce and, of course, great in Mac Daddy.

2 cups vegetable broth or water
1/4 cup all-purpose flour
1 tablespoon olive oil
3 cloves garlic, minced
Pinch of dried thyme (crumbled in your fingers)
1/4 teaspoon salt
Several pinches of freshly ground black pepper
1/8 teaspoon turmeric
3/4 cup nutritional yeast flakes
1 tablespoon fresh lemon juice
1 teaspoon prepared mustard

- Combine the broth and flour in a measuring cup and whisk with a fork until dissolved (a couple of lumps are okay).
- Preheat a small saucepan over medium-low heat. Place the oil and garlic in the pan and gently cook for about 2 minutes, stirring often and being careful not to burn the garlic.
- Add the thyme, salt, and pepper, and cook for about 15 seconds.
- Add the broth, turmeric, and nutritional yeast, and raise the heat to medium.

- Use a whisk to stir constantly. The mixture should start bubbling and thickening in about 3 minutes; if it doesn't, turn the heat a bit higher.

- Once the mixture is bubbling and thickening, stir and cook for about 2 more minutes. Add the lemon juice and mustard. The mixture should resemble a thick, melty cheese.

- Taste for salt (you may need more, depending on how salty your vegetable broth is), turn off the heat, and cover the pan to keep it warm until ready to use. The top might thicken a bit while it sits, but you can just stir it and it will be fine. Serve warm.

From *Veganomicon: The Ultimate Vegan Cookbook* by Isa Chandra Moskowitz and Terry Hope Romero. Used with permission.

Ten Ways to Use Cheezy Sauce

1. In Mac Daddy (see page 109)
2. For nachos
3. For Welsh rarebit (put over toasted bread, cut into triangles)
4. For fondue. Dip bread chunks and veggies into it.
5. Over pasta
6. Over home fried potatoes
7. Over baked tofu, a tomato, veggie Canadian bacon, and an English muffin for tofu benedict
8. Over rice and steamed greens
9. Thin with more broth, add some steamed veggies to it and you have a soup.
10. In and/or over enchiladas

Part Four

Everything in Its Season

In this chapter we will present one day's menu for each of the four seasons. And while you can certainly make any of these breakfasts, lunches, or dinners any time of the year, we thought it would be reassuring to see that vegetarians can eat filling, delicious, easy meals whether the snow is falling or the air conditioning is cranked to the max.

Throughout the summer we hardly use the oven at all. But when the cooler evenings return in the fall, we enjoy the warmth and aroma of baking food. One of Patti's favorite dinners includes lasagna, along with a green salad and a good, crusty bread.

After the seasonal menus, we identify other great meals and suggest menus for a reception or for entertaining.

Winter

Breakfast
- Hot oatmeal with flax seeds, chopped apple, chopped pear, walnuts and cinnamon (See also Luscious Oatmeal, page 46.)
- Whole grain toast with almond butter

Lunch
- Jennifer's Lentil Barley Soup (see page 122)
- Hummus with crudités (radishes, jicama, carrots)

Dinner
- Lasagna with tofu ricotta (see pages 98–100)
- Green salad with fennel and bok choy

WINTER HOLIDAY MEALS

- Lasagna or stuffed shells with roasted veggies and salad and ginger-bread
- Roasted, steamed, or sautéed veggies, flavored and covered with puff pastry
- Scalloped potatoes with a salad (see page 106)
- Stuffed Acorn Squash (see page 104) with a light salad
- Stuffing from acorn squash recipe plus mashed potatoes with gravy (see page 144)

Spring

❦

Breakfast
- Whole grain unsweetened cold cereal in soy, rice, or almond milk, with berries, flax seeds, walnuts
- Whole grain toast with jam
- Scrambled tofu with toast (see page 47)

Lunch
- Cabbage and chickpea soup (see page 62)
- Green salad with sprouts and orange slices

Dinner
- Polenta with pesto (see pages 89 and 78)
- Chopped salad (see page 51)

SPRING "GREEN" CELEBRATIONS

Have any of the below with fresh asparagus to celebrate the coming of Spring!
- Cheddary Cheez Soup (use a variation that adds green to the soup) (see page 64) with Terry's Omega-3 patties (see page 94) garnished with spinach
- Dragon bowl with greens (see page 124) and simple peanut sauce (see page 142)

Spring

- Dragon bowl with veggies (see page 124) and pesto (see page 78)
- Mac Daddy (use variation with greens) (see page 109)

Summer

♨

Breakfast
- Fruit smoothie with banana, berries, peaches, apricots, and orange juice

Lunch
- Mixed green salad with green and yellow zucchini
- Whole grain crackers with red pepper/cashew spread
- Summer soup with a wrap

Dinner
- Burritos with broccoli and salsa (see page 75)
- Aztec salad (see page 49) or corn on the cob

FOODS FOR A PICNIC

- Potato Salad (see page 52) and sandwiches made with fresh sliced veggies and a pesto topping
- Wraps (see page 73)
- Tofu "cottage cheese" and fruit with scones (pages 86 and 112)
- Hummus and veggies (see page 76)
- The "It Doesn't Taste like Tofu" Dip (see page 85)
- Gazpacho (see page 58) plus bread
- Quinoa Salad (see page 53)
- Lentil Salad (see page 54)

Fall

☙

Breakfast
- Easy French toast with maple syrup (see page 45)
- Apple/walnut salad

Lunch
- Broccoli on brown rice with avocado and sesame seeds
- Miso soup (see page 61) with green onions and carrot slices

Dinner
- Indian lentils with broccoli and cauliflower
- Braised kale and collards with garlic and ume plum vinegar

HARVEST CELEBRATIONS

- Stuffed Eggplant (see page 91)
- Mushroom Stroganoff (see page 87) with roasted vegetables
- Stuffed Acorn squash (see page 104) with brussel sprouts
- Baked spaghetti squash with mushrooms and tomato sauce (spaghetti squash bakes in about 30 minutes, simply dig it out of its shell and mix with your favorite sauce)
- Tortilla lasagna (use tortillas instead of lasagna noodles) and stack with your favorite fillings
- Stuff small pumpkins with Jennifer's Lentil Barley soup (see page 122)

When Company Comes for Dinner

We have learned over the years that it is not necessary to work so hard when people are coming to eat: People love the food we serve and it is filling. When entertaining, it is helpful to remember that a few delicious offerings can be quite sufficient.

Your meal choices could include:

- Lasagna plus a big salad plus some Italian bread
- Roasted vegetables with fennel plus tofu steaks
- Baked potatoes with a variety of toppings
- Stuffed eggplants with roasted potatoes
- Use the rich and creamy tofu ricotta and stuff into shells, or mix with steamed spinach and stuff into shells. Serve with a big salad.

During the summer, Carol prepares gazpacho and serves it with the "It Doesn't Taste like Tofu" dip (see page 85) and freshly made croutons.

Every dinner party is made so much more festive with a dessert. Serve the chocolate crème pie (so easy to make) with fresh fruit, or scones topped with nondairy frozen desserts. In the wintertime, serve some warmed gingerbread (you can top it with some warmed applesauce with a little ginger juice added to it). All of the frozen desserts are also delicious on their own or with any baked dessert. Plus, fresh fruit is always refreshing and beautiful.

Ten Tips for Hosting a Reception

1. You can offer a variety of dips and spreads with veggies to dip into them along with crackers and breads. Carol puts the "It Doesn't Taste like Tofu" dip into a hollowed out round bread loaf.
2. Make some wraps (using perhaps roasted red peppers, cucumbers, mushrooms, grated carrots, with a dressing of your choice). Then slice the wraps so that they can be eaten as finger food.
3. For sweets, you can offer either scones or chocolate crème pie or chocolate chocolate chocolate bread.
4. Choose a variety of appetizers (see next page).
5. Buy pre-made guacamole and add chopped up avocado to it. Serve with chips.
6. Make Cheezy sauce (see page 146), add diced tomatoes with green chiles (Rotel is one brand) and serve warm for a great nacho dipping sauce.
7. Buy small mushrooms (cremini or baby Portobellos), cook whole in some broth with garlic for ten to fifteen minutes. Serve with toothpicks.
8. Make (or buy) two hummus variations and place in the same bowl in a yin/yang design (variations found on page 77).
9. Spread peanut butter in collard greens, roll, and cut into thin pieces.
10. Buy a variety of flavored olives and serve on a pretty platter.

Ten Quick Appetizers

1. Spread vegan cream cheese on small bagels, black bread, or Carol's chocolate chocolate chocolate bread. Then spread a thin layer of raspberry jam on top.
2. Braise some sliced fresh mushrooms in olive oil. Add garlic, fresh parsley, salt, and pepper. Cook a little while longer until the garlic is soft.
3. Make bruschetta (cut thick slices of bread, brush with olive oil and broil). Top with some mashed white beans (canned are fine) mixed with minced garlic, olive oil, and sage. Optional: Add some broccoli rabe or kale cooked in olive oil with garlic on top. Or simply put sliced avocado and sundried tomatoes on bruschetta.
4. Stuffed Medjool dates with almonds.
5. Hummus.
6. Steam veggie hot dogs, roll in tortillas with Dijon mustard. Slice.
7. Veggie "meat" balls in a sweet and sour sauce served with toothpicks.
8. Fruit kabobs. Use the small kabob sticks and decoratively place pieces of fruit on them.
9. Steam or roast green and white asparagus and toss lightly with some olive oil, balsamic vinegar, and pepper. Encourage people to eat with their fingers.
10. Crudités with pesto, red pepper cashew spread, salsa, or black bean dip. (See "Quick Dips and Spreads," page 76.)

Visiting the Sick, and Other Times that You Bring Food to Someone

※

Foods you can take to a sick friend:
- Miso soup that you warm when you arrive there (see page 61)
- Gingerbread (see page 116)
- Jennifer's Lentil Barley soup (see page 122)
- Carol's Chocolate Chocolate Chocolate Bread (see page 117)
- Other comfort foods (see page 32)

If you are going to wait in the hospital while someone is being operated on, you can take some scones (see page 112). People who are waiting have often been in the hospital for a long time that day, and usually are too nervous or worried to take a break to eat. Carol has found the scones always provide just the right kind of nourishment.

If you are taking food to a friend who is in the hospital or just recently released, you might take:
- applesauce (you could add: raisins, cinnamon, a hint of ginger juice)
- rice cakes or rice crackers
- a mild vegetable broth
- herb teas
- a smoothie (with just the frozen banana, soymilk, and a little cinnammon).
- Bananas in soy yogurt with cinammon and a little maple syrup

Ten Foods for Hosting a Brunch

Brunches can be so much fun; especially because all the preparation is done beforehand and so you can relax with your guests. If you have a chafing dish kicking around in a closet, unused for years, here's a chance to enjoy its ability to keep food warm on a table.

1. Make a big fruit salad. Add some dried fruit to it if you wish.
2. Make French toast ahead of time, dust with cinnamon and keep warm in the oven (see page 45).
3. Make a double amount of tofu scramble, and keep warm in the chafing dish. Have tortillas nearby, and olives, avocado, and salsa, and encourage people to make their own migas.
4. Roasted potatoes
5. For a tasty drink: buy a seedless watermelon, and purée it with lots of ice and some fresh mint.
6. For breads: if you don't want to bake anything, buy some artisan breads at the store, slice, and place a variety of jams nearby.
7. Make those irresistible scones (see page 112).
8. If not scones, biscuits (see page 48).
9. If not scones or biscuits, chocolate bread (see page 117).
10. Hummus made with eggplant (see variation on page 77) or "It Doesn't Taste like Tofu" dip on page 85, served with pita.

Birthdays

For a child's birthday party:
- Mac Daddy (see page 109)
- Veggie hot dogs with baked beans and corn on the cob
- Pita pizzas (with children picking their own topping)
- Make your own taco bar: have chopped lettuce, tomatoes, avocados, chopped up tofu steaks, chopped red and green peppers, and salsa
- Desserts: chocolate crème pie (see page 115)

For a birthday celebration for an adult, why not a wrapped dish? Yes, twice-baked potatoes are a wonderful addition to any birthday celebration, and they come wrapped in potato skin or foil.

BASIC TWICE-BAKED POTATOES

- Bake the potatoes and let them cool.
- Without destroying the outer skin, scoop out the flesh into a mixing bowl.
- Add your favorite filling and mix.
- Spoon back into the potato skin. If you want a crusty taste, leave as is. Or wrap in aluminum foil. Refrigerate.
- About thirty minutes before the birthday celebration, return them to a 400 degree oven and bake.

- Possible fillings for twice-baked potatoes: steamed and mashed broccoli, carrots, spinach, mixed together or on their own; sautéed mushrooms; scrambled tofu (see page 47); cooked lentils; Terry's Omega-3 patties (crumbled) (see page 94)
- Possible sauces to mix with veggies or use on their own: cheezy sauce (see page 146); holiday fat-free sauce (see page 144); Chick Cheez (see page 72)
- Desserts: Scones (see page 112) with fruit salad or scones split in half with nondairy ice cream, or chocolate bread (see page 117) sandwiches made with raspberry jam and Tofutti better than cream cheese

Part Five

Thinking and Feeling Like a Vegetarian, if You Want To...

Many of us began our vegetarian adventure purely for health reasons. A vegetarian diet is in keeping with the recommendations of a growing number of medical experts: the cancer specialists, heart specialists, kidney specialists, liver specialists, diabetes specialists, and the obesity specialists. Because it does not put additional stress on the body; because it is naturally high in fiber, antioxidants, and phytochemicals; because it is naturally devoid of cholesterol, low in saturated and trans fats, and actually contributes to the body's overall health, a vast majority of health professionals heartily endorse a diet based on whole, natural foods.

We might have begun our vegetarian adventure for health reasons only, but as we became more at home in the world of plant-based eating, we saw that the benefits of eating from the earth extended far beyond our personal improvements in health. The planet's air, water, and topsoil all benefit when humans choose a vegetarian diet. And of course, the ten billion land animals who are slaughtered for food in the U.S. every year stand to benefit as well. So many of us who started out just wanting to reduce our risk of heart disease, cancer, diabetes, obesity, stomach and digestive disorders, and other health threats have found ourselves making choices to honor other living beings and to help preserve the resources that are necessary to grow our food and support life on Earth.

There Are Only Two Food Groups

🍐

Think of it this way: there are only two food groups: foods from the animal kingdom and foods from the plant kingdom. Just about every food from the plant kingdom is good for us, and just about every food from the animal kingdom is harmful. Here's why:

Foods of animal origin (including fish, pork, lamb, chicken, turkey, beef, milk, cheese, yogurt, eggs) are naturally high in fat, naturally high in saturated fat, and naturally high in cholesterol. These same foods are devoid of fiber.

Foods from the plant kingdom (including whole grains, vegetables,

Animal-Based Foods	Plant-Based Foods
• Devoid of fiber	• High in fiber
• High in cholesterol	• Virtually devoid of cholesterol
• High in fat	• Low in fat
• High in saturated fat	• Virtually devoid of saturated fat
• Leach out calcium	• Supplies calcium
• Without complex carbohydrates	• Rich in complex carbohydrates
• Devoid of antioxidants	• Rich in antioxidants
• Devoid of phytochemicals	• Rich in phytochemicals

fruits, and legumes) are naturally high in fiber, naturally low in fat, virtually devoid of cholesterol, and virtually devoid of saturated fat. (The only exceptions—plant foods that are high in fat, but still contain virtually no cholesterol—can be counted on one hand: avocados, nuts, olives, coconut, and hearts of palm. And even most of these have health-supporting properties that no animal-based food can rival.)

This means that eating like a vegetarian—even if you don't want to become one—is the easiest way to cut fat, eliminate cholesterol, and increase fiber.

Furthermore, plants are loaded with disease-fighting compounds. The same components that protect plants naturally from sun damage and insects also offer protection to people who eat these plants. The risk for many cancers, heart disease, diabetes, osteoporosis, and other conditions—ranging from constipation to gout—can all be reduced simply by including an abundance of colorful foods from the plant kingdom.

Virtually every month, another study discovers that a component of some vegetable or fruit is a powerful fighter in the war against disease. Lycopene (found in tomatoes, berries, watermelon) may reduce the risk of prostate cancer. Lutein (found in spinach, broccoli, kale, collards, parsley) fights heart disease and age-related macular degeneration. Isothiocyanates (found in cabbage) can help reduce the risk of lung cancer.

Diseases of Excess

Most people in developed countries today do not suffer from beriberi, scurvy, rickets, or other diseases of deficiency. If we are eating enough calories to maintain our weight—not a challenge in twenty-first-century America—it is virtually impossible to have a protein deficiency. What we *are* suffering from and dying from are *diseases of excess*. Think about gout, cancer, arterial sclerosis, heart attacks, strokes, osteoporosis, obesity, irritable bowel syndrome, and diabetes. These are all, in part, the result of too much cholesterol, too many toxins, too much saturated fat, too much animal protein, too many calories, and not enough fiber.

The only component of food that we have too little of today is fiber. That's why laxatives and digestive aids are among the bestselling over-the-counter medicines in the drug store. Fiber plays a vital role in keeping us healthy. It works as a trash collector, gathering up what is harmful and taking it out every time we have a bowel movement. Fiber helps keep our digestive systems running smoothly. It takes bad cholesterol and free radicals (altered cells that are precursors to cancer) out of the body. Fiber helps transport many other toxins out of the body, too. Enough fiber ensures that our bowel movements are regular.

Two of our favorite books go into greater detail about why vegetables are so good for us.

Joel Fuhrman, MD devised a simple, yet extraordinarily powerful formula for optimal health that he describes in his book *Eat To Live*:

$$Health = \frac{Nutrients}{Calories}$$

In other words, health is predicted by your nutrient intake divided by your calorie intake. Dr. Fuhrman calls this the nutrient-density issue, and it's an extremely simple, profound, and health-promoting way to look at any food and any diet. In Dr. Fuhrman's words, "Every food can be evaluated using this formula. Once you begin to learn which foods make the grade—by having a high proportion of nutrients to calories—you are on your way to lifelong weight control and improved health. Eating large quantities of high-nutrient foods is the secret to optimal health and permanent weight control."

When we learned that the foods with the very highest ratio of nutrients to calories are vegetables, we were inspired to eat more vegetables—even though we'd already been vegetarians for a very long time!

Another book that details the myriad benefits of eating more vegetables for improved health is *The Color Code* by James Joseph, Anne Underwood, and Daniel Nadeau. Organizing food by its color, the book talks about the thousands of macro- and micro-nutrients in all colorful vegetables. It explains how each color and each food within that color group has a strong effect on everything from eyesight to heart disease, brain function to cancer. They write:

> One of the most exciting lessons to come out of all this new research is the realization that the greatest number of healthful compounds can be found in the most colorful foods. . . . Virtually all fruits and vegetables—pale and vibrant alike—have something to recommend them. But vegetables that are darker not only have more antioxidant pigments, they often have more vitamins as well.

Nutrient-Dense Food

One of the reasons this formula for health works is that when you eat nutrient dense foods until you're full, there is no room left for the nutrient deficient foods that are laden with calories but devoid of any benefit—and often toxic—to your body.

We have seen this work in our own lives, and we've seen countless other people lose weight, lower their cholesterol, reverse their heart disease, decrease their headaches, eliminate their constipation and heart burn, and increase their energy, just by eating more vegetables! It's as simple as it sounds, and as profound as you can imagine.

The only intelligent way to talk about all of the nutrients in a food is to do it by nutrient density of calories. Often, people talk about *per weight* or *per volume* when they talk about how much of something is in a food, instead of *per calorie*. One of the reasons we are obese in our nation is because people are told how many grams are in something not by calorie, but by volume or weight. That is meaningless. We consume calories. Two percent milk isn't actually 2% fat; it's about 30% fat *by calorie.*

To fill up on fried foods and animal foods and milk and cheese, you have to eat tons of them to feel full, which would mean taking in way too many calories. If you were going to eat 100 calories of broccoli, the broccoli would weigh 10.6 ounces (about three cups of broccoli). But if you were going to eat 100 calories of sirloin steak, it would weigh .84 ounces. Which would make you feel full faster and longer? Less than one ounce of steak or three cups of broccoli?

What about Calcium?

Calcium is vitally important. But to look for calcium in a high protein diet from animal foods will not ensure that you retain enough calcium. It is protein itself that is causing the problem. Too much protein in the diet is turning the blood ever so slightly acidic. Just as your temperature wants to be about 98.6°F, your blood wants to maintain a steady balance between acidity and alkalinity. Every time you eat animal protein, your blood turns a little more acidic than your body is comfortable with. The body wants to find something that will neutralize that acid, so it looks around for something that can neutralize acid. Where does it find such a substance? The calcium in our bones does the trick.

Calcium neutralizes acid; that is why Tums, a popular antacid, is made of calcium. The body, always wanting to balance its acid/alkalinity says, "Hey, here's some anti-acid right here in the bones, how convenient!" So it takes calcium out of the bones, where you want it to be, and runs it through the bloodstream. Then it is excreted in your urine. In one study, women were fed large amounts of protein. No matter how much calcium these women took in over the course of the diet, they were in negative calcium balance; that is, they were excreting more calcium than they were retaining. In fact, because most of the world doesn't have the high protein consumption we do and subsequently does not have the leaching of calcium that results from consuming so much protein, the World Health Organization recently lowered the amount of calcium that it says we need.

The idea of taking calcium in a form that is naturally high in protein (such as milk) is counterproductive. But the ratio of protein and calcium in plant foods is ideal.

Consider the cases of osteoporosis you have seen in your life—a grandmother, an aunt, a mother. Most of the women who now have osteoporosis were following the recommendations for protein and calcium formulated by the United States Department of Agriculture. The countries that have the highest intake of dairy—Western European countries, Scandinavian countries, North American countries, and Australia—are the same countries that have the highest bone-fracture rates in the world. In the famous Harvard nurses' studies, the people who drank the most milk had the highest bone-fracture rate. (Because there is a connection between milk drinking and prostate cancer, men should think twice about drinking cow's milk, too.)

This does not mean that you do not need calcium. We all need calcium. But it does mean that the scary information about the unmet calcium needs of vegetarians and vegans is not true.

Compare the calcium in broccoli versus beef:

- For 100 calories of broccoli (about three cups), there are 322 milligrams of calcium
- For 100 calories of sirloin steak (less than one ounce), there are 2.4 milligrams

When it comes to calcium, broccoli is more than 150 times better. Did you know that even among nonvegetarians, almost 40% of the calcium in the American diet comes from plants?

Milk Is Not the Perfect Food

Most of us grew up believing, and many of us still believe, that milk is the perfect food. In fact, it is—if you are a baby and you are drinking milk from your mother's breast. Milk is miraculous! Its nutrient composition changes day to day to keep up with the changing nutritional needs of the baby. A newborn needs a different balance among fat, carbohydrate, and protein than a six-month-old needs. And a one-year-old needs a different balance than a nine-month-old. A mother's body knows when it gave birth, and the milk for that mother's offspring changes to meet the changing needs of the child. Mother's milk continues to be the perfect food for that particular mother's child as the child grows to about three years old. (Of course, after six months a child requires solid foods in addition to mothers' milk. But the milk is still an ideal food for babies and toddlers, even when it is not the entire diet.)

This ability to change its nutritional makeup is true not only for human mothers' milk, but for the milk of every mammal as well. Horses, camels, oxen, dogs, giraffes, cats, and, yes, even cows produce the ideal food, changing day by day for the offspring of their own species. Cows at birth weigh about 60 pounds. They are designed to grow to 600 pounds, doubling their weight in about a month, more than four times faster than a human baby doubles its birth weight. Cows' milk is the perfect food to help calves do this. It has bovine growth hormones and nutrients perfectly designed for baby cows. Human breast milk has human growth hormones and nutrients perfectly designed to help human babies grow.

When human babies drink cows' milk, they are ingesting foreign proteins, foreign antibodies, and foreign nutrients, all of which may not be recognized by the human baby's body.

According to Dr. John McDougall, human infants deprived of the advantages of human breast milk have:

- Two to four times the risk of sudden infant death syndrome (crib death)
- More than 60 times the risk of pneumonia in the first three months of life
- Ten times the risk of hospitalization during their first year
- Reduced intelligence as measured by IQ score
- Behavioral and speech difficulties
- An increased chance of suffering from infections, asthma, eczema, Type I diabetes, and cancer (lymphoma and leukemia) in early life
- A greater risk of heart disease, obesity, diabetes, multiple sclerosis, food allergies, ulcerative colitis, and Crohn's disease later in life (McDougall newsletter, April 2003)

Adding Colors and Crunch; Variety and Abundance

Even if you are going to eat fish or flesh, you still need to eat a lot of vegetables, both raw and cooked, because of their incredible protective benefits. Think of it as adding *colors* and *crunch* to your diet. Make sure that at least one or two meals a day has many colors or lots of crunch, or both.

Instead of saying to yourself, "I need to leave something out of my diet to add color and crunch to it," you can see this process as simply introducing new things into your diet. These new things are whole grains, vegetables, legumes, and fruit.

If you follow this idea that in adding colors and crunch to your diet, you are adding new things rather than eliminating old ones, at some point you will find that you enjoy everything about your meal. Indeed, at some point, you might discover that grains, vegetables, legumes, and fruits have become the center of your meals. And you'll have learned how delicious, creative, and varied your meals can be.

In addition to colors and crunch, you will want to ensure that you are eating a *variety* and *abundance* of these whole, natural, plant-based foods. This will guarantee that you aren't hungry.

Variety is important. Whenever we discover a new recipe we like, we tend to make it over and over again. But even the most delicious and nutritious meal can become monotonous. Don't get on a kick where all you eat is one favorite food. Try something new. Aim to fill your plate with different colors. Green, orange, red, and yellow foods are packed with nutrients and are the most attractive. Go to a farmer's market and pick something new that is colorful: Radicchio or red cabbage in a green salad is gorgeous. Or add a yellow pepper or corn to black beans for contrast.

Eat a salad at the start of lunch or dinner. That way, you fill up on the most nutrient dense foods and leave less room for the less nutrient dense foods later in the meal.

We have suggested looking at food as falling into two simple groups: plant-based foods or animal-based foods. The Physicians' Committee for Responsible Medicine (PCRM) has further divided the plant-based food group into four subgroups to help us plan what to eat. These four food groups include whole grains, fruits, vegetables, and legumes. If we had to choose only one group within the plant food group to focus on, it would surely be vegetables, because so many nutrients, compounds, and health benefits are found in just about every one you can name. But focusing only on vegetables would be misleading. Fruits, legumes, and whole grains are equally important in our diets. By eating a variety and an abundance of foods from all the plant-based food groups we will easily take in all the nutrients we need, including protein, calcium, and iron.

If the only thing you did were to increase the number of plant-based foods in your diet, you would certainly notice a change in how you feel. But if you focus especially on certain foods from the plant kingdom, you will reap the most beneficial rewards. In the next section we discuss these special foods.

PCRM's division of the plant-based food group into whole grains, fruits, vegetables, and legumes can be helpful. But it's still just fine—and easier—to think about there being only two food groups and then to eat a variety and abundance from the plant-based food group.

Three Foods We Love Best

A parent should never admit to having a favorite child, and as vegetarians we are loath to admit to having favorite foods from the plant kingdom. We love them all!

But from a health standpoint there are three kinds of food that stand out as particular shining stars in the vegetarian firmament—three foods that reduce the risk for cancer and heart disease, provide plenty of calcium, and show more and more evidence of being a "magic bullet" for staying well:

- cruciferous vegetables
- legumes
- dark, leafy greens

Cruciferous vegetables are the ones that smell strong when they are cooked: broccoli, cauliflower, Brussels sprouts, cabbage, and kale. These foods have been shown to regulate a complex enzyme system that defends the body against cancer, especially lung, stomach, bladder, prostate, and colorectal cancer.

Legumes are another disease-fighting food that deserves more attention in the typical American diet. According to the Linus Pauling Institute, "Not only are legumes excellent sources of essential minerals, they are rich in dietary fiber and other phytochemicals that may affect health. Soybeans have attracted the most scientific interest, mainly because they are a unique source of phytoestrogens known as isoflavones. Although other legumes lack isoflavones, they also represent unique packages of nutrients and phytochemicals that may work synergistically to reduce chronic disease risk."

Legumes? "Uh oh," you think, "I have to learn something new and this is what has kept me from eating like a vegetarian!" But you don't have to learn something new. A more familiar term for *legumes* is beans. If you have had hummus, you have had legumes. If you have had lentil soup or black bean soup or chili, you have had legumes. There are countless ways to incorporate delicious legumes into our diets.

TEN COMMON FOODS MADE FROM LEGUMES

1. Hummus
2. Lentil soup
3. Black bean dip
4. Vegetarian chili
5. Three bean salad
6. Split pea soup
7. Indian dhal
8. Edamame (soybeans in their pods)
9. Peanuts (not a real nut, but a legume)
10. Green peas

Our third favorite food is dark, leafy greens—including kale, collards, mustard greens, beet greens, broccoli, and bok choy (notice that the last one is both a dark, leafy green *and* a cruciferous vegetable!). These dark, leafy greens are among the best sources of calcium on the planet. Horses, oxen, elephants, camels, and other animals who have been used as beasts of burden for millennia are all strong vegetarians who get their calcium from dark leafy greens. Patti saw elephants when she was in Africa a few years ago. What impressed her was that they did not walk on a path, they created one as they walked by eating any branches in their way! They eat continually and walk continually, eating leafy greens (and woody branches) as they go. And the older elephants do not have weak bones! See the list on page 8 for how to include more dark, leafy greens in your diet.

If you develop the habit of filling up first with a salad, and if you start to add some legumes or some broccoli or some kale or some collard greens to that salad, you'll be well on your way to the healthiest nutrition-packed diet there is.

Vegetables Are Tops (and Stems and Roots)

How astounding that humans eat just about every part of plants: stems (celery), roots (carrots), leaves (spinach, kale), fruit (you name it), seeds (sesame, pumpkin, sunflower), flowers (cauliflower, broccoli). What's more, plant foods are ideal foods for humans. And while we don't eat every part of every plant, with some foods we do—such as beets and beet greens, or celery stalks and their leaves! Lettuce, spinach, kale, chard, and collards invite us to eat the entire plant. In Japanese cultures, many kinds of seaweed are often eaten in their entirety as well.

If you haven't included fresh vegetables in your kitchen, we'd like to invite you to become familiar with them. Start with the simplest vegetables, such as carrots and celery. Many supermarkets sell ready-to-eat, trimmed celery spears and pre-washed baby carrots. You can call them "crudités" and feel fancy, or call them "dipping sticks" and feel very down home. Either way, if you dip them into hummus or guacamole, baba ghanoush or salsa (all available pre-made in most natural food stores and increasingly available in supermarkets), you are on your way to including more vegetables in your diet. As you feel familiar with these common vegetables, you may want to add radishes, jicama, zucchini, or cucumber spears for dipping into your food of choice. For visual contrast, you can add a few olives on top of a plate of mixed veggies.

Another quick and easy way to include more veggies, especially the powerhouse cruciferous veggies, is to steam and mash some broccoli and/or cauliflower. If you prepare this "mash" as most folks prepare egg salad (with chopped celery, onion, pickle, mustard or eggless mayo), you will have a scrumptious filler for sandwiches, cucumber "boats," or sweet peppers. You can also serve a scoop of this "mashed salad" on top of a bed of lettuce greens for a cholesterol-free alternative to egg salad.

The best way to become more familiar with new vegetables is to try one new vegetable each week. You can ask a grocer, or a farmer at a farmer's market, what she recommends; or you can pick up something colorful and foreign to you and see what you can do with it. A computer search on any vegetable will lead you to dozens, if not hundreds, of recipes and suggestions about preparing and eating each new discovery.

Shopping for produce should always be an adventure in color! We often get compliments on the rainbow of colors in our shopping baskets. If you shop the produce section first and fill your basket with a variety of colors, you will be able to eat like a vegetarian. How marvelous that in eating like a vegetarian you will be including the healthiest foods in the planet in your diet.

The Animal Connection

M ost people like animals. Very few people would admit to the statement, "No, I don't like animals." Even fewer people would go out of their way to hurt animals. But the beef, chicken, and pork industries along with the egg and dairy industries have made it very easy for you *not* to go out of your way to hurt animals.

It's not in the scope of this book to go into excruciating detail, but in summary we do want you to know . . .

- Animals raised for food in this country live under unspeakably horrid conditions.
- For female animals, their lives are ones of confinement, artificial insemination, pregnancy, separation from their offspring, and more pregnancy. Male offspring are often killed immediately or while still babies.
- Most animals are kept confined during their lives. They live their whole lives without seeing sky.
- Animals are often mutilated during their lives.
- Deformity of animals' bodies occurs because they have been bred to have unnatural features.
- By the way they are restrained, animals' natural instincts are thwarted. They are unable to stretch, scratch at the ground, root for food, or care for their young.

- They are shipped to slaughter without water, food, fresh air, or space to turn, lie down, or walk.
- Their deaths are gruesome. In addition, slaughterhouses boast the most injuries and the highest rate of employee turnover of any industry in the United States.

This is sad information and it doesn't get any less sad once you know it. The more we write about it and the more we read about it, it stays sad. But we have learned that being alert to how animals experience their lives has made our lives not just more humane, but more human. It is okay to feel grief when learning about these facts and thinking about the lives of farmed animals; but that grief does not incapacitate us. It teaches us that we are connected.

To feel like a vegetarian, it helps to acknowledge that farmed animals live miserable lives. Most of the chickens who lay eggs and the cows whose milk we drink are bred for maximum production and are deformed in the process. Even "humanely raised" chickens come from hatcheries where the male chicks are killed as fast as they hatch.

Cows, like all mammals, will produce milk only when they have given birth, so they must be kept pregnant to keep their milk supply flowing. Unlike most humans, cows don't get to enjoy courtship and sex, but are artificially inseminated two to three months after giving birth. This process begins when the cow is 15 to 18 months old and continues for years.

When the calf is born, if she is a female, she, too, will be raised as a dairy cow, confined in a stall, continually made pregnant, and mechanically milked throughout the day. The milk that was intended for her calf will be taken from her, as will the calf, as she was from her own mother.

If the calf is a male, he is of no value to the dairy farmer, so he is sold for slaughter after a short life in a stall too small for him to turn around.

Cows with unnaturally large udders frequently develop mastitis and are in pain much of the time. They are both lactating and pregnant, so that their bodies' nutritional resources are diverted from their own needs to the growing of a baby and the production of milk.

The lives of dairy cows and their young are among the most awful lives imaginable. Many vegetarians sincerely believe that it would be better to continue eating meat than to continue eating dairy foods because the lives of dairy cows are so much longer and more tortured than the still miserable, but not quite as miserable, lives of beef cattle.

The birds we count on for eggs live on factory farms, crowded six to a battery cage, no larger than a page of newspaper. Their legs grow deformed from standing on wire-cage floors and their feathers wear off from being pushed against the wire sides of the cage. They cannot spread their wings, establish a natural pecking order, or dust bathe. They cannot exercise any of the natural behaviors that throughout millennia hens have exhibited. Because of their crowding, infections are common—and costly—to the business. So antibiotics are frequently added to the birds' food. And because crowded birds are frustrated in not being able to scrabble in the dirt for their food, they pick at one another in the crowded cage. To reduce the damage, the "farmers" sear off the beaks of chicks.

And speaking of chicks, just as male offspring of dairy cows are useless to dairy farmers so male chicks are of no financial benefit to the egg farmer. But unlike the male offspring of cows who are sold off as veal calves, the newly hatched male chicks are suffocated or thrown alive into a large, garbage-disposal-type machine, and ground up. And all egg-lay-ing operations get their chicks from hatcheries where this practice is common.

Recently, "organically raised" farmed animals have been receiving a lot of consumer attention. Unfortunately, it is not possible to guarantee that one will be consuming only animals who have been less badly treated. Even "free-range" eggs may be produced under difficult situations; the hens are not in cages, but are still crowded within large, closed-in buildings. Moreover, "free-range" chickens and "organic" eggs come from chickens whose lives began in the hatcheries we described above. Besides the difficulty sometimes in confirming what is meant by the term "organic" meat, eggs, and milk, one central problem will always remain: the animals still die.

We know that images of suffering animals are not appetizing ones, and that it can be most unpleasant to learn of the suffering in the lives and deaths of animals. Nevertheless, we want to be truthful about why so many people become vegetarians in the first place and why so many vegetarians decide to leave eggs and dairy out of their diets. Since we don't need as much protein as we've been led to believe and, in any case, it is abundant in plant foods; and since calcium is readily available in dark green vegetables, sesame seeds, and countless other plant-based foods; health issues support the decision to be humane in one's diet. We can look in the face of one chicken or one cow and remember the billions of suffering birds and cows; we can face the facts and find it in our hearts to make more thoughtful food choices.

Many people who came to vegetarian eating did so for health reasons, but once they were committed to that way of eating they were then willing to look at the industries that produce animal foods. Whereas people who are supporting those industries prefer a "don't look, don't see, don't hear" policy, once you stop eating the product of those industries, it's easier to look at the conditions under which animals are bred and raised and killed. And then most people who *became* vegetarians for health reasons realize they wish to *stay* vegetarians because they do not want to support systematic suffering. They not only find they are able to learn about farmed animals, but they find they can respond to the fact that the conditions under which farmed animals live and die are horrendous. They no longer need to live in denial of what is going on behind closed doors. Overcoming the institutionalized denial helps us open our hearts to compassion. We cannot live fully, love fully, or act with integrity when we willfully refuse to learn about and respond to so much suffering.

Animals suffer because eating meat, dairy, and eggs are human habits. People are accustomed to the taste of animal-based foods. But vegetarians have discovered that we can develop new habits. We find it easier and more authentic to broaden and change our tastes than to continue supporting the breeding, confining, mutilating, and slaughtering of farmed animals.

In the face of so much human and animal suffering, it is important to remember that we can take steps to reduce it. Know that every meal in which you choose not to eat animal products is a step to reducing suffering in the world. You certainly don't have to become a vegan or a vegetarian. But if you ate like one—even just for one meal a day—your action would have a tremendous impact in the lives of farmed animals.

A Sense of Connectedness

🍐

In his wonderful book *The World Peace Diet*, Will Tuttle says, "Food is not only a fundamental necessity; it is also a primary symbol in the shared inner life of every human culture, including our own." There are so many issues related to food—from trucking tomatoes over long distances, to the use of fossil fuels in meat production, to factory farming, fish farming, the depletion of the ocean by fishing fleets that are virtual factories at sea, to how small farmers and farm workers are treated. Corporate domination of the world's food supply is changing the way people and countries can and cannot feed themselves with life-supporting foods. What passes for the health industry in the United States is not a health industry at all, but an industry that repairs bad health. Rather than addressing all these issues in a piecemeal way, getting involved with food directly through changing one's diet can address all the issues at once.

Food is a form of connection, and eating like a vegetarian widens the circle of life to which we feel connected. Vegetarians and those who eat like vegetarians are making life-affirming choices that broaden our world view, our sense of connection to all living things, and our culinary repertoire.

If you feel overwhelmed by the world's problems, and you are sick of hearing about global warming, oceans being denuded, rivers being polluted, and topsoil disappearing . . . , if you are exhausted by all the groups that petition for your assistance, you need to know that becoming aware of food issues makes the picture more focused. The picture becomes more focused precisely because eating is one of the most basic things we do; it has one of the greatest impacts on each of us and on the world around us, too.

If you were asked to choose which is best: a diet that is good for your health, or a diet that is beneficial to the environment, or a diet that re-establishes a more just relationship with animals—that would be a tough choice. By beginning to eat like a vegetarian you can choose all three at once—no difficult decisions are necessary.

When eating like a vegetarian, you are taking positive steps toward creating the kind of world we'd all like to see: one with less suffering, for humans and animals; one with fewer wrappers from processed foods littering our cities; one that causes less ill-health. By eating like a vegetarian, you are working for a world with less stench, more rich topsoil, vibrant oceans, and more forests.

Being aware of food issues helps us address issues of global justice, water pollution, health and nutrition, and disease.

We like to think that eating well includes nourishing the spirit, nourishing the world, and nourishing the body. And always because of our decision, we are called back to the truly important things—caring and responding to others and enjoying life.

Dr. Dean Ornish observes that it is sometimes easier to make a big change than to make many little ones. But it's often scary making big changes. By eating like a vegetarian, you are making small changes that have a big impact. Each meal in which you do not eat animals or animal products, you are caring for yourself, domesticated animals, and the planet. Each vegetarian meal forges connections. Each meal is a small change helping to make a big change.

Looking at food issues makes us realize that we are connected to one another and to the Earth. The need for food is one of the few things that every human being has in common with every other human being. Everybody eats, from the day we are born to the day we die. Eating connects us with our ancestors, our families, our neighbors, and our Earth. It connects us also with the nonhuman animals with whom we share the Earth. Feeling connected, we prefer to think of our fellow Earthlings as beings and friends rather than breakfast, lunch, and dinner.

Vegetarianism
Eating for Life Not for a Fad

🍐

Vegetarianism is not a fad diet. It is a way to eat for life that any lab technician who sees your blood panel would approve of.

A fad diet is short term, something one goes on between now and one's high school reunion.

A vegetarian diet isn't a fad diet because you can be on it forever and there is no downside. Fad diets are dangerous not only physiologically, but psychologically. They teach us not to love ourselves, not to love our bodies, and they put too much emphasis on outer appearance. Even though vegetarian diets naturally tend to keep you slim, most vegetarians don't have this as their goal; it is just a side effect. Most vegetarians are more concerned with inner and outer health and the well being of animals than with outward appearances only.

People who are always dieting often have a bad self-image. Generally, it can be hard to find a vegetarian with low self-image because it takes integrity and courage to become and remain a vegetarian.

The only strict rule that vegetarians believe in is to try, in every situation, to do the least harm. Other than that, vegetarianism is not actually in any way about restriction; it's about making choices for the most good to others and the least harm. We do not have any desire to eat meat. It's not that we can't, or that meat is restricted, or that we don't have a choice. We do have a choice and we choose not to eat meat.

When they become parents, people may have a new sense of accountability. They may tell themselves, "I can't go skateboarding anymore; I can't go skydiving; I can't ride a motorcycle without a helmet." Parents make decisions like these because they want to be there for their child. They don't want to take unnecessary risks that would harm them because the biggest risk would be that they would not be there for the child.

Likewise, parents don't usually buy motorcycles for their children when they turn sixteen. The natural instinct of loving people is to protect the people they love. Nobody would call a naturally protective parent "restricted."

People don't say to parents who exhibit such protective behavior toward themselves and their children, "Oh God, you're no fun anymore, you can't have a good time anymore." People understand that parents are being protective and why.

Just so, vegetarianism is not a restrictive diet. We have become aware of our relationships to other creatures. We can still have fun, we can still have a good time; we have simply decided not to engage in acts of consumption that put others at risk.

Many people hold to vegetarian stereotypes. But, you don't have to fight the stereotypes. You don't even have to call yourself a vegetarian. You can tell people you are eating more:

- Plant foods
- High fiber foods
- Zero-cholesterol foods
- Nutrient-dense foods
- Cancer-preventing foods
- Heart-healthy foods

- Powerhouse foods
- Superhero foods (like dark leafy greens)

Plant-based food is virtually every color of the rainbow except brown; if you don't want to call yourself a vegetarian, say you are on an anti-brown diet.

You can eat like a vegetarian without ever having to be one!

Thankfulness

Patti reports that when she was growing up, the only time she expressed gratitude for her food was at summer camp. "We said a cheer before eating: 'Rub a dub dub. Thanks for the grub. Yay God!' We laughed to turn a traditional grace into a typical camp cheer, yet it was a reminder that our food came from somewhere else. It didn't just show up magically in the dining hall." That experience caused Patti to realize something very important: "I'd always thought that saying grace before meals, as I witnessed it in movies, was something only Christians did. My own family, Reform Jews, seldom said words of thanks before eating, except to the cook. Even on Thanksgiving, we spoke only about the abundance of food on Grandma's table, never the source of the food itself. It was only after I became a vegetarian that I saw the beauty of my connection to food and discovered the calm and sense of well being that saying 'thank you' could add to a meal."

When we take a moment to feel and acknowledge our gratitude for the food we are about to eat, we might also want to acknowledge the source of our food. This can be a much more pleasant undertaking when farmers and grocers are involved than when slaughterers and butchers are part of our food's past.

Vegetarians like to think about eating well as a way to nourish the spirit as well as the body. More than simply being about the quality of food or its health benefits, eating well includes eating with a feeling of peace, well being, and acceptance of and gratitude for the path the food took to reach our plates.

Many vegetarians find that our eating pleasure is enhanced when we take a moment to express our gratitude before eating. Whether alone or with others, we thank the farmers, workers, truck drivers, grocery store clerks, and the home or restaurant cooks who were all instrumental in bringing our food to the table. We can do this silently or aloud, and we can include our gratitude also to the sun, rain, soil, earthworms, and other forces that brought our food from the earth. Whether or not we believe in God or follow a particular religion, we can enjoy the fruits of gratitude by expressing thanks for the colors, flavors, and nourishment that food provides.

A Healthy, Happy Life

W̶hen it comes to food, vegetarians do not live lives of deprivation! You may think we do because you have watched us at barbecues, at family events where meat takes center stage, or in restaurants that were not of our own choosing. But vegetarians enjoy abundantly good food at home and in restaurants—when we choose the menu! There are hundreds of restaurants around the world that cater to vegetarians and countless more every year that include delicious choices for vegetarians. When you see us at our own dinner parties, potluck dinners, picnics, barbecues, and at restaurants that know how to prepare plant-based meals, you see people eating well, enjoying magnificent food, and choosing from a larger variety of foods than most meat eaters can imagine. As Mr. Rogers, in his succinct wisdom pointed out, "There are many more varieties of vegetables than there are of meats."

Vegetarians are some of the happiest people we know and some of the most effective at helping to heal the world.

We are happy because we have some modicum of control over issues that are important to us.

People who are forced to eat a vegetarian diet because their doctor tells them they have to are the only grumpy vegetarians we've ever met. If they can be made to see what a huge gift that diet really is and what an exciting culinary opportunity it offers, they frequently go from being grumpy to being joyful about the many positive contributions their diet is making to their own health and the world.

Many vegetarians tend to be very happy people because we know we are having a positive effect in a world that sometimes seems beyond our control. We are taking concrete steps to minimize a number of diseases—diabetes, heart disease, cancer—and to reduce environmental degradation.

If you pay attention to what you take in, you will notice how it affects the quality of your life. This is true not only for food, but also in what magazines you allow into your house, what radio or television programming you listen to or watch, and what people you choose to spend time with.

Many vegetarians have become conscious of how everything we allow into our bodies and our minds affects our health and well being. Turning down or getting rid of excess noise, obnoxious talk show blather, toxic work environments, and other unhealthy habits is often as nourishing as adding more healthful foods and eliminating toxic foods. There are different kinds of food; we feed ourselves aurally and visually even more frequently than we feed ourselves with food. We feed ourselves with the friendships we form and the environments we create for ourselves.

And vegetarians know this: The health industry is really found in farmers' markets. The health industry is composed of the broccoli growers, the grain merchants, the fruit pickers.

If you think of food as a life-support system instead of as a form of entertainment, joy comes from that life-support system turning into a life-*delight* system.

People who make a full commitment to healthful living have fewer complaints than those who eliminate only red meat and don't really examine the wider issues surrounding food.

Happy vegetarians are taking positive steps to create the kind of world we'd like to see: one with less suffering, for humans and animals; one with less need for health care insurance (though we are very much in favor of universal health care!).

The vegetarians we know are some of the most compassionate people in the world. We don't make the distinction between the welfare of animals and the welfare of human beings because the same choices can alleviate human and animal suffering. The same choices clean up our water and our air, our colons and our blood vessels.

Vegetarians we know are the activists who are lobbying for improvement to land, the rights of animals to live natural lives, access to healthful foods in underserved neighborhoods, a return to balance in our oceans—and dozens of other concerns that affect the entire population of the planet. Furthermore, the vegetarians we know are the most kind and generous people we are acquainted with—with their time and their money in purely human endeavors as well. When we hear someone call into a radio show to complain that vegetarians care more for animals than for people, we shake our heads in sadness and disbelief. The truth is that vegetarians tend to be very active in every sort of people-helping organization. We tend to get more publicity for our work for animals; but, in truth, most of us are quick to volunteer wherever we are needed, and we try to alleviate human suffering as well as animal suffering wherever we can.

The vegetarians we know are writing letters to newspapers, calling our senators, educating others about what really works to promote health. It just so happens that we know that eating a vegetarian diet is a very practical, easy, and delicious way to do that—in addition to all other methods and causes we support.

The changes we have each undergone since becoming vegetarian have expressed themselves in surprising areas—we find ourselves more active, sleeping better, playing harder, and being happier and more confident that our choices can help to change the world for the better. Knowing that we are not part of the problem but part of the solution, our happiness is continually expanding.

Conclusion

We hope we have persuaded you to eat like a vegetarian more often. Perhaps even to think like one from time to time. In any event, we end this book as we began it, with thanks to you for taking the time to read it. We wish you good health and joy as you eat like a vegetarian—even if you never want to be one.

Appendix 1

Resources for Eating, Thinking, and Feeling like a Vegetarian

TEN HELPFUL WEBSITES

1. HappyCow.net (To find vegetarian-friendly restaurants worldwide.)
2. VegCooking.com (PETA's best recipes)
3. CompassionateCooks.com (Colleen Patrick-Goudreau's wonderful website. Sign up for her free newsletter and read her blogs.)
4. PCRM.org (Free recipes, good works, and free Vegetarian Starter kit)
5. VegKitchen.com (recipes, nutrition advice, and more from Nava Atlas)
6. www.drmcdougall.com (Great articles and recipes. Sign up for this physician's free newsletter.)
7. www.TheChinaStudy.com (Wonderful overview of a wonderful and important book.)

8. Google.com (Search on Vegan Thanksgiving, Vegan Meatloaf, or vegan anything else. You will be delighted with the tens of thousands of recipes that are available for free.)

9. www.FatFreeVegan.com (Not all recipes are entirely fat-free, but many are and they are terrific.)

10. www.VegSource.com (Articles, information and recipes plus links to dozens of great vegetarian sites; sort of a *Readers' Digest* for all things vegetarian.)

TEN (PLUS TWO) BOOKS TO INCLUDE IN YOUR LIBRARY

1. *The Color Code* by James A. Joseph, PhD, Daniel A. Nadeau, MD, and Anne Underwood

2. *Eat to Live* by Joel Fuhrman, MD

3. *Living Among Meat Eaters* by Carol J. Adams

4. *The Vegetarian Way* by Virginia Messina, RD and Mark Messina, PhD

5. *Healthy Eating for Life* from Physicians Committee for Responsible Medicine (Series includes books about diabetes, children, women, cancer.)

6. *Food For Life* by Neal Barnard, MD

7. *The China Study* by T. Colin Campbell

8. *Becoming Vegetarian* by Brenda Davis, RD and Vesanto Melina, MS, RD.

9. *Becoming Vegan* by Brenda Davis, RD and Vesanto Melina, MS, RD.

10. *The Truth About Breast Cancer* by Joseph Keon, PhD

11. *The Food Revolution* by John Robbins

12. *Mad Cowboy* by Howard Lyman and Glen Merzer

Ten Cookbook Authors You Can Trust

1. Jennifer Raymond, author of *The Peaceful Palate* and *Fat-Free and Easy*
2. Isa Chandra Moskowitz and Terry Hope Romero, authors of *Veganomicon: The Ultimate Vegan Cookbook*
3. Robin Robertson, author of *Vegan Planet* and *Vegetarian Meat and Potatoes Cookbook*
4. John A. McDougall and Mary McDougall authors of *The McDougall Quick and Easy Cookbook*
5. Jo Stepaniak, author of *The Ultimate Uncheese Cookbook, Vegan Vittles*, and *The Saucy Vegetarian*
6. PETA, author of *The Compassionate Cook* (especially good for children)
7. Colleen Patrick-Goudreau, the author of *The Joy of Vegan Baking*
8. Tanya Barnard & Sarah Kramer, authors of *How It All Vegan!* and *The Garden Of Vegan*
9. Bryanna Clark Grogan, author of *The (Almost) No Fat Cookbook* and *The (Almost) No Fat Holiday Cookbook*
10. Ken Bergeron, author of *Professional Vegetarian Cooking*

Peace on Earth

Isn't man an amazing animal? He kills wildlife—birds, kangaroos, deer, all kinds of cats, coyotes, beavers, groundhogs, mice, foxes, and dingoes—by the million in order to protect his domestic animals and their feed.

Then he kills domestic animals by the billion and eats them. This in turn kills man by the million, because eating all those animals leads to degenerative—and fatal—health conditions like heart disease, kidney disease, and cancer.

So then man tortures and kills millions more animals to look for cures for these diseases.

Elsewhere, millions of other human beings are being killed by hunger and malnutrition because food they could eat is being used to fatten domestic animals.

Meanwhile, some people are dying of sad laughter at the absurdity of man, who kills so easily and so violently, and once a year sends out cards praying for "Peace on Earth."

C. David Coats, *Old MacDonald's Factory Farm*
Used with permission.

Appendix 2

Guide to Ingredients

Baba Ghanoush. An eggplant dip made from roasted eggplant, garlic, tahini, and lemon.

Bok Choy. A green leafy vegetable often used in Chinese cooking.

Bosc. A variety of pear.

Broccoli rabe. A variety of broccoli, which many find more tender than broccoli itself.

Chapatti. An Indian flatbread.

Daikon. A radish.

Dulse. A sea vegetable; often sprinkled on foods instead of salt.

Edamame. Soybeans in their pod, a very popular appetizer in Japanese restaurants; available frozen in many supermarkets.

Ener-G Egg Replacer. The brand name of a powder that one can use in place of eggs. Its ingredients include potato starch, tapioca flour, dairy-free calcium lactate, calcium carbonate, citric acid, and carbohydrate gum. Mixing 1 1/2 teaspoons egg replacer with two tablespoons water creates the equivalent of one egg. One can also use bananas, soft tofu, arrowroot powder, or cornstarch as a binder in baked goods.

Gomasio. A mixture of ground sesame seeds and salt, used as a condiment.

Hoisin. A sweet, spicy sauce used in Chinese cooking.

Hummus. A spread easily made from chickpeas, tahini, garlic, and lemon juice.

Jicama. A sweet white vegetable that when peeled and sliced is delicious in salads and for dipping.

Matzoh. A cracker eaten on Passover, or any time of year; available in ground form for making matzoh balls.

Mirin. A sweet Japanese cooking wine made from sweet rice. The best-quality mirin is made from sweet rice, rice *koji*, and water with no added sugar, alcohol, or fermenting agents.

Miso. A fermented soybean paste that adds flavor to sauces and soups. Some misos are made solely from soybeans and salt. Others are made from soybeans, salt, and a grain such as rice or barley, or legumes such as chickpeas. It is a fine source of high-quality protein. It provides a salty flavor, and can mimic, at times, Parmesan cheese in some recipes (see, for instance, the pesto recipe). Avoid boiling miso once you have added it to a dish because intense heat will destroy its healthful enzymes. Keep refrigerated. Found in health food stores, natural food stores, and Asian food stores.

Napa cabbage. A light green cabbage, almost resembling lettuce.

Nutritional Yeast Flakes. Refers to Red Star formula (T6635+) nutritional yeast flakes. Do not confuse it with brewer's yeast. Red Star nutritional yeast is an inactive yeast; it does not produce fermenting effects on baked goods. Instead, it is a rich source of B-complex vitamins, specifically riboflavin, niacin, thiamin, and biotin. It also provides protein when added to foods. If your local health food store does not carry it, it can be ordered from The Mail Order Catalog, P. O. Box 180, Summertown, TN 38483, 1-800-695-2241. Jo Stepaniak's *The Nutritional Yeast Cookbook* and *The Uncheese Cookbook* provide numerous scrumptious recipes incorporating nutritional yeast flakes.

Quinoa. A grain that cooks in only fifteen minutes (but must be rinsed before cooking or will taste bitter). Makes a great base for a salad or as an addition to any salad.

Sucanat. Stands for SUgar CAne NATural. It is an evaporated sugar cane juice. It contains more minerals, trace elements, and vitamins than table sugar. It adds a depth of flavor to baked goods and other items that call for a dry sweetener. You can substitute it for refined sugar, one cup for one cup.

Tahini. A paste or liquid made from ground sesame seeds.

Tamari Soy Sauce. A fermented soy sauce made from soybeans, salt, water, and a starter called *koji*. It is nothing like commercial soy sauce, indebted to caramel for its dark brown color and corn syrup for its sweetness. Tamari soy sauce's fermentation occurs through the introduction of a soybean starter. If you cannot eat fermented foods, you may enjoy the tasty alternative of Bragg's Liquid Aminos.

Tempeh. A meat substitute made from fermented soybeans and a whole grain. Steam for 20 minutes and use crumbled instead of tuna in tuna fish salad, or cooked in some tamari as a base for a Reuben sandwich.

Textured Vegetable Protein. TVP is texturized vegetable protein. It is made from soy flour. After the soybean oil has been extracted, cooked under pressure, extruded, and dried, the result is a dense, textured food that is chewy and "meatlike." It is sold in granules, flakes, chunks, or slices. When rehydrated, the granules resemble ground "beef" and the chunks have the texture and appearance of chunks of "meat." Especially when cooked in certain ways, it is often mistaken for meat and can be substituted for meat, such as "hamburger," in recipes like "sloppy joes." TVP is an excellent source of protein and fiber, and has zero cholesterol. The initials are the registered trademark of the Archer Daniels Midland Company.

Tofu. An inexpensive, versatile, high-quality protein, that is cholesterol-free, rich in calcium, and made from soybeans. It is made in a process similar to making cheese: soymilk is coagulated, drained, and then the curds are pressed into a cake. (Home tofu kits are now available.) The fear of tofu is due, in part, to its blandness. In fact, its "blandness" is what makes it so versatile because of its ability to absorb a variety of flavors. Tofu is labeled according to its water content. The less water it contains, the firmer the tofu is and the more likely it is to hold its shape in cooking. Regular tofu is packed in water, and usually found in plastic tubs in the refrigerator section of a health foods store; but now can be found in the produce section of more and more supermarkets. Keep it refrigerated. Silken tofu is creamy, smooth, and available in aseptic boxes that do not require refrigeration. If you are frying or baking tofu, use regular tofu. If you are using tofu in baked goods, creamy soups, puddings, or cream pies, use silken tofu.

Turbinado. Unrefined raw sugar similar in appearance to brown sugar.

Ume vinegar. A tasty, salty Japanese vinegar that you can find in many natural food stores.

Acknowledgments

Patti thanks Fran Zitner, Stan Rosenfeld, Connie Hatch, Dominique Blanchard, Jennifer Raymond, and everyone who has attended her cooking classes over the year. Your support and encouragement have been invaluable.

Carol thanks Bruce Buchanan, her children, Douglas and Benjamin, Shirley Wilkes Johnson for teaching her so much about vegetarian cooking, and for adapting the bread recipe, and her friends Carol Mai, Christina Nakhoda, Susan Allison, and Pat Davis, for letting her experiment upon them.

Together we thank the people of Lantern Books, especially Martin Rowe and Kara Davis, for ongoing support.

And we thank one another for a great collaboration.

Copyright Acknowledgments

The authors thank and acknowledge the following authors and publishers for permission to use these recipes herein:

Ken Bergeron for "Roasted Vegetables with Garlic and Fennel Seeds" from *Professional Vegetarian Cooking* (New York: Wiley, 1999).

Jennifer Raymond for "Aztec Salad," "Cabbage and Chickpea Soup," "Broccoli Burritos," "Stuffed Eggplants," "Gingerbread," "Lentil Barley Soup," and "Simple Peanut Sauce," from *The Peaceful Palate* (Summertown, Tenn.: Book Publishing Company, 1996).

Jo Stepaniak and Book Publishing Company for permission to use "Chick Cheez" from *The Ultimate Uncheese Cookbook* (2005), "Cheddary Cheez Soup," from *Vegan Vittles* (1996), and "Cashew Cream Sauce," from *The Saucy Vegetarian* (2000).

Isa Chandra Moskowitz and Terry Hope Romero for permission to use "Mac Daddy" and the accompanying "Cheesy Sauce" from *Veganomicon: The Ultimate Vegan Cookbook* (New York: Marlowe & Company, 2007).

David Coats for permission to reprint "Peace on Earth" from *Old MacDonald's Factory Farm* (New York: Continuum, 1989).

Additionally, all registered® and trademarked™ product brand names are used with our appreciation of the product, and promotion of their use.

About the Authors

Carol J. Adams has been a vegetarian since 1974, and has raised two vegetarian children, who continue as happy vegetarians in their adulthood. She is the author of the classic *The Sexual Politics of Meat: A Feminist-Vegetarian Critical Theory* (Continuum), *Living among Meat-Eaters* (Lantern), *The Inner Art of Vegetarianism* (Lantern), *Prayers for Animals* (Continuum), and several other books. She has also edited several anthologies on the connection between feminism and animal issues. She always keeps the ingredients for scones in her house because, as she says, "You never know when someone will need comfort food—and sometimes it's me!"

Patti Breitman has been a vegetarian since 1985. She is the director of The Marin Vegetarian Education Group in Marin County, CA, (www.MarinVEG.org) and a former columnist for *VegNews* magazine. Patti is the co-author, with Connie Hatch, of *How to Say No Without Feeling Guilty* (Broadway Books). She shares her skill by teaching vegetarian cooking classes, and shares her lack of skill by singing in a community chorus, and tap dancing, which she enjoys tremendously.

Index

Of Related Interest from Lantern Books

The Inner Art of Vegetarianism
Spiritual Practices for Body and Soul
Carol Adams

"True to her heart, Carol Adams boldly continues the fight against prejudice in general and one form of prejudice in particular. It is a prejudice so deeply rooted and ingrained in us that we hardly notice. It is our prejudice against animals."—**Sharon Gannon**, Jivamukti Yoga Center

101 Reasons Why I'm a Vegetarian
Pamela Rice

"If you've ever been curious about vegetarians and why they eat the way they do, Pam Rice is the woman to tell you. Without sentimentality or preaching, she provides a clear and thoughtful understanding of one of the most important choices a person can make. You don't have to be a vegetarian to benefit from this book. You only need to care about your health and the health of our planet."—**John Robbins**

The Lantern Vegan Family Cookbook
Brian McCarthy

"*The Vegan Family Cookbook* will be warmly welcomed in any vegan household with hungry little mouths to feed. With over 400 family-geared recipes, the book is a gem of a collection of tasty, familiar dishes that will make it a treasured volume in any kitchen."—**VegParadise.com**

To order, visit www.lanternbooks.com.